Rethinking
Human Resources

RLP
PROFESSIONAL SERIES

Red Letter Publishing, San Francisco
Copyright © 2015 by Red Letter Publishing and below-named authors.
All rights reserved.

The official list of contributing authors is as follows (by last name):

Rebecca Barnes-Hogg
Teri Cirillo (co-author with Emily Hosea)
Nichole Cobb
Jocelyn Davis
Kristin Dunlevy
JC Gibson
Sherri Harbsmeier
Michele Fantt Harris
Emily Hosea (co-author with Teri Cirillo)
Nikki R. Jackson
Cheryl Jekiel
Maurie McGarvey
Jeff Nally
Dave Phillips
Laura Hlavacek Rabideau
Bob Smith

Book typeset by Kevin Williamson
Cover design by Kevin Williamson
Cover image © Jkerrigan | Dreamstime.com

Created in the United States of America

21 20 19 18 17 16 15 1 2 3 4 5

ISBN 978-0-9864371-9-9

Acknowledgements
from the Publishers

First, we owe our thanks to the authors in this anthology. We love having an opportunity to share their messages and their stories, and we cherish it all the more because we get a chance to know the people behind them. Their wisdom and insight, which you can find for yourself in the coming pages, was matched in turn by character and professionalism. It has been a privilege to work with all of them.

Many thanks also to Sharon Armstrong of the SAA Trainers and Consultants Network, a free referral service for HR, OD, trainers, coaches, and keynote speakers. Sharon is a HR consultant and author, and she was very helpful to us as we began to develop this anthology. She can be reached at (202) 333-0644 or online at www.trainersandconsultants.net.

Lastly, we would like to thank the authors of the recent *What's Next in Human Resources*, a "prequel" anthology published by Greyden Press, for their continuing efforts to build a robust community of forward-thinking Human Resources professionals through writing and publication.

This anthology is centered upon a simple idea: that the daily work of Human Resources can be bigger, better, more meaningful, and more impactful. The authors bring their perspectives on Human Resources and how it can live up to new dreams in the coming years of change. We're proud to share their visions with you.

— *Cathy Fyock and Kevin Williamson*

Contents

Rebecca Barnes-Hogg

Hiring Rerouted:
Use a GPS Mindset to Drive Your Hiring Strategy

Organizations cannot afford to hire blindly. Every hire is critical, and making a bad hiring decision can cost your business thousands of dollars and many hours of your time.

Before we had GPS systems, if you took a wrong turn and got lost while traveling, you experienced that distressing feeling when you realized you made a mistake. You had to get out a paper map to figure out where you were and how to reach your destination. Today, GPS technology makes it easier to reach your destination and avoid wrong turns. A "GPS mindset" provides a navigational tool to guide your hiring decisions.

The labor market is highly competitive and will be even more competitive in the future. According to a report from the Conference Board, "The retirement of baby boomers will create a shortage of skilled workers in mature economies worldwide." Everyone is competing for a limited supply of talented people, and now is not the time for hiring mistakes.

Millennials are now the largest generation represented in the workforce—and yet 53% of hiring managers say it is difficult to find and retain Millennials. According to Manpower's 2015 talent shortage survey, 38% of employers are having difficulty filling jobs. Hiring managers, like sales managers, need to know their candidates and appeal to what matters most to them so they can respond to your call to action: taking a job working for your business. Millennials tend to value doing something that is enjoyable or that makes a difference, while Boomers tend to value learning new things and earning the highest possible paycheck.

If you are tired of missing out on the talented people you need, you're not alone. Many businesses struggle with hiring. They copy what others have done or they follow a formula from an "expert," but these rarely work because each business, including yours, has unique needs. Trying to "think like Google or Apple" rarely works well for a small business with limited resources.

The hardest part is knowing where to begin. As Stephen Covey says, "Begin with the end in mind." A "GPS mindset" provides the framework for good direction.

With a GPS device, you begin by entering a specific destination, then a specific starting point. Then you can choose options based on your needs—fastest route, shortest route, fewest tolls, no highways, and so forth. It's your responsibility to be specific and thorough with the information you give the GPS; if you enter vague start or end points, or don't adjust the options to reflect your needs, you can't get the best results from the GPS—and may run into problems. Anyone who has driven around cities knows that a lack of detail in programming your GPS can take you on some journeys. Not all of them are fun; some can be terrifying, slow and time-consuming, or costly.

The lost time and resources rarely amount to much in the case of GPS miscalculations—a few minutes usually, an unexpected toll sometimes. But the stakes are much higher with hiring, and there is much more to lose. CareerBuilder surveys illuminate some of the ways that a bad hire can have cascading effects through the business:

- 27% of employers say a single bad hire costs them $50,000 or more.
- 66% of employers have been affected by a bad hire.
- 48% of CEOs report that they lost money because of inefficient recruiting practices.
- 60% of CEOs report the inability to find qualified candidates is preventing the company from reaching their full potential.

A lack of clarity about your destination results in bad hiring decisions. Let's get out our GPS system and get to work programming it well.

Step One: Enter a very specific destination. This is your job description. Many businesses either don't write job descriptions or have job descriptions so outdated they're irrelevant. Remember that a good job description is clear in two areas: skills and attitudes. The job description shows both the outcomes and the skills required of the person to achieve those outcomes. Remember that there is a reason every position in your business exists; be very clear about those reasons and get them down on paper. Most companies write job descriptions that are based on a list of tasks—in effect, a "to-do" list. If you use a GPS mindset and create a destination list, you are more clearly able to see the skills and behaviors required.

Be clear about skills tied to outcomes. Here's an illustration of being more clear about your needs.

A doggie spa (in older days called a kennel) had a very difficult time staffing their receptionist position. They had constant turnover and the business owner could not get the receptionist to increase customer spending when they boarded their dogs. When she changed how she viewed the position and focused on her final "destination"—the outcome of increasing customer spending—she understood that a receptionist was not the right job description. She needed a salesperson. When she hired a sales-oriented person, she reached her destination: increased customer spending and no turnover in the position, a win-win scenario.

In addition to strong technical skills, successful people have certain attitudes and be-haviors that fit your business. You can hire the best technical person available, but if they do not possess the attitudes and behaviors you need to be successful, it can be a painful experience. We have all struggled with someone with great skills who just never quite fit in.

A great example of this is Riley Csernica, a Millennial I had the opportunity to hear speak at a TEDx event in Charleston. As she was finishing her degree in Biomedical Engineer-ing at Clemson University, she went to her first job interview. Riley had a plan and was going to do whatever it took to get the job. She crushed the interview. She shared her ideas, showed her critical thinking and analytical skills, and was enthusiastic throughout.

The interviewers told Riley how impressed they were with her. She appeared to have the technical skills, enthusiasm, great ideas exploding out of her head, and so much vision for their company—and because of that, they *could not* hire her.

The company needed someone who could stand at the end of a production line and check little boxes to make sure their products met specifications. The interviewer recognized that Riley would hate that job. She would be miserable if that were what she had to do every day. This is a great example of being exceptionally clear about what you need; hiring Riley only because she was technically proficient would have been a bad fit for both the business and Riley. The relationship would have ended in disappointment for both parties. Because of the company's clarity on their final "destination," Riley felt great about not getting the job. Hopefully, that company went on to hire someone who enjoyed checking boxes.

Step Two: Enter the starting point. Take a good look at your business and identify your high performers and low performers. Write down the qualities of your high performers and your low performers. Be very specific. If you do not know what differentiates a high performer from a low performer, how will you know if you are hiring a high performer?

Prepare for your "trip" by planning to upgrade your low performers to high perform-ers, perhaps by reassigning them to positions that are a better match for their skills and attitudes—or, if necessary, by planning for their transition out of your organization.

Step Three: Begin following the directions. Occasionally, things don't go as planned and something unexpected occurs. On the road, you might have car trouble, traffic de-lays, road construction, or any number of other obstacles—but using the GPS, you can find a solution or an alternate route to bypass the problems. When you are hiring, you also need to plan for some miscalculations and obstacles, just like on the road.

Let's pause a moment and look at the hiring process in more detail. You are clear now about where you are and where you need to go. You will need a strategy to get you from your starting point to your destination. Who are the types of people looking for this type of work? Where will you find them? How will you articulate a value proposition that will appeal to them? How will you attract those people to your business? This is where your GPS mindset will start showing you all the great things you have to offer along your route.

You will need to clearly state the value a candidate gets by working for your business—not a one-size-fits-all pitch. Suppose you're a manufacturer who is seeking a customer service rep. The customer service rep would be responsible for all the minutiae involved in their sales transactions: tracking numbers, shipping confirmations, delivery dates, sample requests, order entry, and on and on. This person would also need to build relationships with customers and create a bond. This requires two very distinct skillsets: attention to detail when performing repetitive tasks and communication and relationship building. You might have been recruiting for the position without success for many years. But when you clarify the tasks and the personality traits required for success, you can find the right fit for the position—and the employee can become a valuable team member and grow her career with the company.

When you travel, you have different choices for restaurants, entertainment, shopping, and so forth. You have these choices in your business as well. Your mission and vision will be the guiding principles that help you attract the right people. You need people who share those same values and a passion for your mission. Most companies start by telling candidates how great they are to work for, but they fail to tell candidates what they can expect in return. A dull job description makes people less likely to apply for jobs, and if you are using a job description to attract workers, it had better be clearly focused on the "destination" and selling the candidate on the position.

Start by appealing to their interests just as you would if you were trying to sell your product to a customer. For Millennials, remember that they favor an enjoyable job or one where they can make a difference. Appealing to employee interests is such a simple tactic, and its profits can be great—yet many businesses aren't thinking of hiring in this way.

This strategy worked for a nonprofit who had a difficult time filling an entry-level position on their editorial staff. When they changed their job posting to appeal to someone who shared their mission, presented the value of the work product, and appealed to what was most interesting to the right candidate, they were able to hire a talented Millennial who was passionate about good writing and possessed an eagle eye for clarity of message and thought. That was four years ago, and that Millennial has become one of their most valuable team members.

Another "GPS tactic" is to focus on the options the system gives you for how you want to reach a certain destination. Just as you can choose the shortest route, fastest route, avoid highways, avoid tolls, or other criteria on the road, there will also be similar factors for jobs that merit attention. Just as most people default to major highways for their routes, many jobs default to standard educational requirements, such as a Bachelor's degree—but there are other factors to consider.

We know Millennials value doing something enjoyable or that makes a difference. Unfortunately, we apply a Boomer mindset that a college education is required to teach necessary skills. Millennials don't operate by that assumption; they are a generation raised on instant information and, as a result, self-directed learning. If they want to learn something, they download a book, watch a YouTube video, or visit an online community filled with experts ready to share their knowledge.

Consider the story of Will Jamieson. He is a college student who built seven apps and is part owner of a business worth 500 million dollars. In his TEDx talk, "College: Necessary, But Insufficient," he talks about how, in eighth grade, he taught himself how to program his TI-83 calculator by reading the manual, and that was his entrance to the world of coding. He loves the freedom of writing code to make something new and innovative (his form of art). His dream was to be one of the first guys who made an iPhone app, so Will bought a book on iPhone development and went to work.

For Will, the "return on investment" of learning on his own couldn't be measured in dollars; putting himself into the experience was its own value for him. That gave Will the courage to leave his comfort zone and put himself into situations where he could learn everything he needed to expand and run a business. He would not have this experience if he had not created the experience. Isn't it time we created a route that does not default to college education as the only way to prepare for a career? While formal education plays an important role, it should not limit your choices. More and more, if you considering only college graduates, you may be overlooking the most creative, innovative, and skilled candidates, especially among Millennials.

The GPS mindset gives you a new framework for making the right hiring decisions. It gives you a way to navigate through the hiring process to avoid hiring people you will later regret. If you break it down into a systematic process, you can hire confidently, with more clarity, and make the right hiring decisions for your business needs.

As a reminder of everything we have covered on our journey, here is a quick recap:

- Have a clear destination. Begin with the end in mind and get specific about the desired outcomes.
- Know your starting point. Be clear about what behaviors, attitudes, and skills constitute a high performer and a low performer.
- Map your route. Know what you have to offer that will attract high performers to your business. Follow your route and plan for the unexpected. Be willing to adapt and change along the way to keep on course.
- Hire with confidence. You have a clear starting and ending point with a plan to get you there.

You are equipped with the tools and resources that give you clarity to plan your hiring strategy. The GPS mindset provides insights that direct your actions to arrive at the results your business needs.

Enjoy your journey. Stay in touch with me and get all the navigational tools you need at www.yoloinsights.com.

Quick References

Link to Conference Board report:
https://www.conference-board.org/topics/publicationdetail.cfm?publicationid=2819

Link to Riley Csernica's TEDx talk:
http://tedxtalks.ted.com/video/Zero-Equals-One-Creating-A-Busi

Link to Will Jamieson's TEDx talk:
http://tedxtalks.ted.com/video/College-Necessary-But-Insuffici

Rebecca Barnes-Hogg

SPHR, SHRM-SCP

Rebecca Barnes-Hogg, SPHR, SHRM-SCP, is the founder and lead consultant with YOLO Insights. She is a hiring mentor, recruiting strategist, and Human Resources expert. Rebecca's strength is leveraging her unique and innovative approach to hiring amazing people to help small business owners and entrepreneurs grow their businesses. She shares her approach to hiring through her Right Insights, Right Fit, and Right Choice programs where her services center on what insights small businesses and entrepreneurs need to identify the right fit and make the right choice in their hiring decisions.

Rebecca's personalized approach provides the insights to direct actions to achieve results. Her down-to-earth and fun approach to a frustrating and time-consuming process has allowed her clients to hire the best people. Her programs bring her clients more confidence, less stress, and a bigger profit!

Rebecca has held a variety of HR leadership roles in corporate and non-profit organizations and is a sought-after speaker on a variety of topics related to interviewing and hiring, communication, and teambuilding. Rebecca also writes for industry journals and publications on HR topics.

Rebecca holds an M.A. in Human Resources Management from The George Washington University and a B.S. in Business Management from The National-Louis University. She holds the SPHR certification from HRCI and the SHRM-SCP certification from SHRM.

Teri Cirillo and Emily Hosea

Spark Imagination

Picture this: you are working in Human Resources, People Operations, Human Capital, or whatever your organization calls it, and you are leading the changes in the organization. You are not only generating new ideas, but you are also inspiring others to spark their imaginations for a more creative and engaging experience at work. You are a beacon of light and optimism for your team and your colleagues. People think of you as a lighthouse of imagination because you show the way through murky times and negative thoughts. You don't leave innovation to the traditional "creative types" like R&D or Marketing; you live by the belief that everyone can tap into their imagination and create new ideas, which lead to innovation and success.

Walt Disney once said: "Every child is born blessed with a vivid imagination. But just as a muscle grows flabby with disuse, so the bright imagination of a child pales in later years if he ceases to exercise it." Maybe many of us have lost our strength of imagination, but what if HR led the way in creating a workplace that encouraged and even expected people to exercise their imaginations? If our often-uninspired workplaces are evidence that this faculty is underused, and if Disney was right about imagination (we'd take his word over most others on the subject), just imagine the workplace of the future once our minds have regained this full strength. Imagine that work is a place full of new ideas with a constant stream of innovations that, in turn, are growing the business. How much fun would that be?

If HR takes the lead and creates an environment open for imagination, then people, organizations, and companies will be more innovative and successful. We will describe and give examples of how to tap into your imagination, the benefits of imagination, and how you can attract, welcome, foster, and sustain imagination in your organization.

Defining Imagination

According to the Merriam-Webster Dictionary, imagination is "the act or power of forming a mental image of something not present to the senses or never before wholly perceived in reality." In other words, imagination is your mind picturing something new or different from what you already know.

According to BusinessDictionary, innovation is "the process of translating an idea or invention into a good or service that creates value or for which customers will pay." Put another way, innovation is doing good or making money by putting an idea to work. For this reason, great imaginations lead to great innovations.

> "*Imagination is more important than knowledge. For knowledge is limited to all we now know and understand, while imagination embraces the entire world, and all there ever will be to know and understand.*"
> —Albert Einstein—

We believe that, for imagination to thrive, three critical ingredients must be present and functioning together:

1. An open mind (in the individual and in the organization)
2. Freedom (freedom from threat and worry, whether perceived or real, personal or organizational)
3. Inspiration—which can come from anything, anyone, or any place. For Isaac Newton, it was an apple that led him to develop his theory of gravitation, so you never know.

Ingredients for Imagination

1. Open Mind

Inspiration and imagination require an open mind. You must believe that you and your organization are creative, or can be. Create this mindset by using the tools listed under Inspiration below. Keep yourself as open as possible to all possibilities and ideas. Don't dismiss new ideas too quickly; give them time to process. Allow yourself and others time to experiment and try things out. Try "riffing," or free-form brainstorming by association, to build new ideas. Use "yes, and" when discussing new ideas with others, rather than "yes, but" or "no because"—as we learned from our friends at The Rise Group, an innovative consulting company.

2. Freedom

All people have the capability for freedom of thought. To be inspired, people need to let go of their own perceived or real limitations. Our unconscious mind—which holds onto past experiences, failures, and fears—can be the enemy of freedom of thought by harboring those feelings. According to Dr. Srini Pillay, Harvard psychiatrist and CEO of Neurobusiness Group, people can reframe their thinking to overcome these limitations; they can use techniques such as possibility thinking and mental imaging to create a new outcome.

At a neurocoaching workshop, Dr. Pillay took the participants through a hypothetical situation: could someone earning 100K per year possibly afford a 2-million-dollar home? Even though we knew we were speaking in theory, and even though most of us are op-timistic people, we immediately concluded that this situation would be impossible. We gave real examples of why it wasn't possible based on previous experiences and logic. In turn, Dr. Pillay patiently responded to each of our negative, "impossible" comments with positive possibility comments. It may become obvious, if you get creative, how this situation could work out; however, our automatic responses shut those possibilities out. Just by reframing the thinking and focusing on the positive, we were able to see much more potential in the situation.

Organizations need to allow people to introduce and experiment with new ideas. All levels of the organization should be encouraged to generate ideas for improvements and innovations. This means providing the necessary resources: time, an open environment, and your support.

3. Inspiration

Inspiration for new ideas can come from anywhere, anyone, or any context. It can be something small and simple, or it can be something grand and complex. Whatever it is, it stimulates new emotion or thought.

We've mentioned The Rise Group—since they've been insightful, let's mention their story. In their workshops, they start with the premise that everyone is born creative, and then they help unlock the potential of people through vibrant experiences. They certainly have had some of their own; one of the founding Risers told us a story about a couple of guys he met in a tent at an empty campsite in the middle of nowhere in Iceland—when asked what they were doing in such a remote place they simply stated they were "eating life with a big spoon." This simple phrase stuck for years and when Rise was created they built it into how they ran their business. Their story, in turn, inspired us to think differently about the way we work.

Here's an example of how they helped. They inspired some new innovation in our HR team during a three-minute telephone conversation on how to make a presentation more interesting and meaningful for a large group. The question posed from Rise was this: what if the people "experienced" what your team has to offer instead of watching a traditional PowerPoint presentation?

That was all it took to reframe the thinking on our team. The presentation changed from one person on stage with a PowerPoint to everyone participating, in teams, using props and toys to demonstrate the organization's values. This let the team demonstrate what we could offer to enhance the learning and the business. It was a great success with very positive feedback. Plus, it was a lot more fun for everyone to do an activity together rather than listening to another talking head (or having to be the talking head).

Fortunately, inspiration doesn't need to come from external resources like consultants. It can be found within the organization every day. As an example, one of the international leaders we worked with provided "memorable moments" for his team by taking them to different events or activities at their quarterly meetings. This allowed them to get to know each other informally and be opened up to different types of cultures and experiences. Even just getting people on their feet and having them share in different ways can inspire others and spark ideas.

Finding Imagination

Where do you have your best ideas? What do you notice about the moments when the ideas pop into your head? Many times, we get our best ideas when our minds are detached or when we're just daydreaming.

Here are five simple examples of how you can open your mind, free your thoughts, and keep yourself open to inspiration in your daily life.

1. **Exercise.** Any kind of exercise can get oxygen flowing to the brain. It can be as simple as standing up and taking a walk through the office, taking the stairs, parking further from your office—or, of course, you could have a normal exercise routine.
2. **Practice mindfulness.** To be more precise about it, Merriam-Webster defines mindfulness as "maintaining a nonjudgmental state of heightened or complete awareness of one's thoughts, emotions or experiences on a moment-to-moment basis." At its simplest, this means being aware of what you're thinking and feeling and allowing yourself to be at peace with it. Some ideal activities for mindfulness are yoga, meditation, or even just quiet time. If you're inclined, you can journal your thoughts and dreams. Appreciate beauty in things, whether it's the evening's sunset or some abstract art.
3. **Try something new.** Try a few new recipes; participate in an art or dance class (they usually have something for beginners); go somewhere different for lunch; take a different route to or from work, or even to your desk. Listen to new genres of music, or even learn an instrument. Learn a language if you're feeling bold—and if you want to go somewhere you haven't been, go.
4. **Play and laugh.** Don't take yourself so seriously. Expose yourself to new kinds of humor however you can: YouTube videos, movies, or talk shows (we favor The Tonight Show with Jimmy Fallon, and he tries something new almost every night). Find ways to have fun like kids do; try coloring books, painting, going to the park, shooting water guns, playing laser tag or paintball, whatever strikes you. If you

have kids or pets in your life, let yourself play like a kid with them. While you're at it, go ride a carousel and actually sit on one of the horses.

5. **De-stress.** Breathe! Remember to keep your "oxygen mask mentality" and take care of yourself first as you must. Put your mask on first before you assist others. Find the best ways for you to relax and have some fun. A stressed-out and over-loaded brain won't be easily inspired.

Benefits of Imagination

There can be many obstacles to imagination; however, the benefits well outshine the obstacles. Rather than help you identify all obstacles, which vary from person to person, we're going to help you focus on what benefits you can earn.

Some benefits of a healthy and innovative imagination include:

- More fun for everyone at work and at home
- Creates new ideas, products, and processes which improve the business and inspire external partners
- Improves efficiency, increases profitability, and creates a competitive advantage
- Builds a positive, creative culture and a continuous improvement mindset
- Increases employee growth, engagement, productivity, and satisfaction
- Anticipates and serves the needs of real people—and thus makes the world a better place

Fast Company identified the 50 most innovative companies in the world and what did they all have in common? Imagination! They are all growing and becoming more profitable due to new ideas and new ways of thinking about their business, their customers, their products, and their people. Predictably, Apple, Google, and Tesla all made the list, as did other companies large and small that started with simple but slightly deviant ideas, companies like AnyPerk, Virgin America, Algramo, and Panera.

HR can play an important role in creating opportunities for imagination, which will then create real change in your organization. To frame this discussion, consider: what if Imagination were a person? How would you welcome, develop and retain Imagination?

Attracting Imagination to Your Organization or Team

Building your employer brand to include imagination as a value is one straight and effective way to attract imaginative people. For example, GE's "Imagination at Work" has helped brand them as an innovative company, one that "imagines things that others don't, builds things others can't and delivers outcomes that make the world work better." They show they are open to new and original ideas. (Take a look at their website or watch their tender "Ideas are Scary" commercial.) GE understands that, if you want to find certain qualities in people, sometimes you have to ask.

Every part of the candidate experience could be open to imagination. What if every experience a person had with your organization entertained them or challenged them in some way? What if your website had entertaining videos or skits that demonstrated your values? What if every person in your organization had a positive comment on Glass Door? What if part of the interview process was a team event or scavenger hunt? What if rather than copying other companies' titles, you let people choose their own titles? What if you offered new perks for innovation or other entrepreneurial efforts? What if every person had a real and equal opportunity to be their best at your organization, without bias?

If you examine Fortune's "100 Best Companies to Work For," you can find numerous examples of companies already taking steps that prove that imagination is an essential ingredient in an engaging work culture.

Welcoming and "Onboarding" Imagination

What if you rolled out the red carpet for new employees, and other employees lined up to cheer on these new rock stars? What if you livened up your orientation with something new and unusual that demonstrated your values and culture? What if new employees were mixed with teams of experienced employees to generate ideas for an organization or community project? (What if you captured all the "honeymoon" ideas of new employees while everything was still fresh and unfamiliar to them?)

Quite simply, employees are more likely to leave the organization in the first few months if they do not feel welcomed as part of the team. It is important to ensure employees have a realistic job preview and know what to expect. This is an important part of HR's role.

Fostering and Sustaining Imagination

What if you broke down barriers and enabled interaction at all levels instead of only within the traditional hierarchy? What if you created a place where all people had access to post their ideas? What if the ideas posted inspired others? What if you opened up the opportunity for all employees to attend innovation shows or idea sharing gatherings? What if every person could provide and receive open, honest and respectful feedback (or "feedforward" as described by Marshall Goldsmith in *What Got You Here Won't Get You There*)?

You probably already thought of all of the reasons why many of these won't work, but what if they were possible, and what if they could lead to something?

For employees to remain engaged and inspired, Human Resources plays an essential role in creating the right environment.

For the ultimate good to result, innovators must be able to follow through on ideas, even if they seem futile or far-fetched. What if all the ideas of 50 years ago—or 30 years ago, or 10, or 5—didn't receive the support they did or have the persistence they did? If they'd conceded and resigned their idea to impossibility, we might not have many of the goods that were able to result, in every field from medicine to technology to consumer products. You can start by dignifying simple questions, questions that can improve your life or the lives of the people around you.

Imagination can be fun, simple, and can have real impact on both companies and people. One of the emerging roles of HR is the Imagination Partner, the force that sparks and kindles imagination. Even if you implement one new idea, it can make all the difference for the evolution to a more engaged and innovative culture. If HR takes the lead and creates an environment open for imagination, then both organizations and the people who serve them will be on the road to success.

References & Further Reading

Businessdictionary.com. Web. July 2015.

"GE Ideas are Scary Commercial." MarketmeNot. Web. July 2015.

"Geek Business." Geek Business. Web. July 2015.

Goldsmith, Marshall, and Reiter, Mark. "Practicing Feedforward." *What Got You Here Won't Get You There: How Successful People Become Even More Successful.* First ed. New York, NY: Hyperion, 2007. 170-76. Print.

"Imagination Institute." Imagination Institute. Web. July 2015.

"Imagination: The Number One Tool for Innovation and Creativity | Innovation Management." Innovation Management. Web. July 2015.

Merriam-Webster. Merriam-Webster. Web. July 2015.

"The Neuroscience Of Imagination." Fast Company. 18 Feb. 2014. Web. July 2015. Web.

Pillay, Srinivasan S. Enhancing Leadership and Business Outcomes in a Changing World Perspectives from Brain Science. Apr.-May 2015. Neurocoaching Workshop. Kent State University, Kent, Ohio.

Pillay, Srinivasan S. Your Brain and Business: The Neuroscience of Great Leaders. Upper Saddle River, NJ: FT, 2011. Print.

Schwartz, Brie. "Kelly Clarkson Can't Be Put Down: 'I'm Never Going to Obsess About My Body'" Redbook 14 Apr. 2015: n. pag. Web.

"7 Steps to Positive Self Talk | PickTheBrain | Motivation and Self Improvement." Pick the Brain Motivation and Self Improvement. N.p., 15 July 2008. Web. July 2015.

"6 Changes That Will Make You More Imaginative." Fast Company. N.p., 28 Mar. 2014. Web. July 2015.

"Small Business Imagination Creativity Equals Success." The Open Site Small Business Imagination Creativity Comments. Web. July 2015.

"Why Imagination and Curiosity Matter More Than Ever." The CIO Report RSS. Web. July 2015.

"The World's 50 Most Innovative Companies." Fast Company. Web.

Teri Cirillo

SPHR, SHRM

Teri Cirillo has been leading HR for companies, including Fortune 100 and 500, for over twenty years. She has been a leader in the Wine and Spirits industry for over 14 years and is currently the VP, Human Resources Americas for Treasury Wine Estates in Napa, California. She has vast experience leading HR for start-up, high performance, and turnaround organizations. She was also the HR lead for mergers & acquisitions and business divestitures.

Teri is a business-focused, insightful Global Human Resource Executive who creates and implements strategies that drive performance and international growth. She is a recognized expert in talent assessment, executive coaching, and leadership development. She builds high-performing teams that deliver outstanding results across the globe.

Teri became a certified Senior Professional in Human Resources (SPHR) in 2002. She is a member of Society of Human Resource Management (SHRM) and is a certified coach in Neurocoaching and the Goldsmith Stakeholder Centered Coaching Process. She holds a Bachelor of Science in Psychology from Northern Michigan University and a Master of Human Resources and Labor Relations from Michigan State University.

Teri is a Leadership Mendocino (California) and Leadership Louisville (Kentucky) alumni and volunteers for AMPED (Academy of Music Production Education and Development), Junior Achievement, Habitat for Humanity and nonprofits' boards.

Teri and her husband have three boys and one dog.

ABOUT THE AUTHOR
Emily Hosea

Emily Hosea is a retired Human Resources Compensation Professional with over 25 years of Human Resources experience. She has volunteered over 15 years for Home of the Innocents Human Resources Committee, and is a member of SHRM, and is a Certified Compensation Professional by World at Work. Emily enjoys the creative process, whether it be in creative brainstorming ideas at work, learning new ways to have fun at home, or taking part in this anthology. You may reach her at EHosea1@gmail.com.

Nichole Cobb

Embracing Inclusion

Earlier this year, I gave a presentation to management pertaining to diversity initiatives and legal requirements. Part of the presentation discussed why all companies need a diverse workforce, yet still one of the managers walked out of the meeting saying, "Basically, then, we are checking the box."

Phrases like "checking the box" create an image for applicants, employees, and supervisors within the company; is this the mindset that CEOs or Presidents want their business to portray? In the changing Human Resources (HR) worldview, three factors—technology, globalization, and a multigenerational workforce—will force business to embrace inclusion. Once this happens, the organization's performance and level of innovation will increase. Let's look at each matter individually and its impact on the corporate world.

Technology

What an amazing world of technology we live in today. Common though it is, take a moment and think back to your parents, grandparents, and great-grandparents and what they had. Think back on your own early years; I grew up watching a black-and-white television with three channels. Yes, there was a time when we only had three channels and they didn't broadcast after midnight; there was a time without cell phones (and a time when one landline was commonly shared with other households). When I was in the military, instant messaging didn't yet exist (much less Skype or FaceTime), so it was not unusual for me to have no contact with my family for six months or longer.

Technology has closed many gaps and, in making communications more global, has made the world seem smaller and more familiar. Automation allows personnel in different countries, continents, and time zones to strategize product issues or brainstorm new ideas as though they were in the same room; it has made phenomena like crowd sourcing and work swarming (using social media to find a solution to a business problem) possible.

Globalization

Can anyone doubt that we are a global world? Predications indicate that 55 percent of global GDP will originate in developing countries in the coming years. Many US businesses either outsource or have moved manufacturing to third-world countries (though the future may see some of this business moved back to the US due to wage hikes in countries like China). Some of us work for businesses that don't intend to become an international company, but we still may need to utilize workers from around the world in future ventures.

Multigenerational Workforce

Human Resources must lead the challenge of embracing a multigenerational workforce and manage (potentially) five generations of workers, through their differences and similarities, then focus them all on the company's mission. Traditionalists, Baby Boomers, Generation X (Gen X), Millennials (Gen Y) and Digital Natives (Gen Z) are our multigenerational workforce, and no two groups are exactly alike.

Not only do we have to incorporate various age groups, but we have to consider that we come from different cultures and ethnicities, life experiences, sexual and gender identities, values, spirituality, work experiences, and disabilities. The workforce population of the future will be markedly different from the ones we've seen in years recently past:

- Current studies suggest we will need to fill 13.5 million job vacancies in the next ten years, but only 7 million young people will leave school with the skills, abilities, and knowledge to supply the gap.
- Half of the Baby Boomer workforce plans to continue to work past retirement age, with 18 percent planning to work into their seventies.
- Minorities will collectively constitute more than half of the US population.
- In the next 20 years, approximately one billion women will enter the global workforce and the majority will be more educated than their male counterparts.
- Individuals with disabilities are the majority minority making up 20 percent of the populace, but 80 percent are unemployed.

Workplace diversity will be evolving fast; we don't have a choice but to recognize and respond to this, especially as the global consumer base comes equally more varied. HR must spearhead and challenge executives and managers to **embrace** the inclusion of all human characteristics, to accept them with some enthusiasm and optimism.

E—ENGAGE executive leadership, managers and employees. Is your firm truly all-inclusive or does it simply comply with what the laws and regulations require of it? Do your senior leaders talk about diversity and inclusion and say that we need to do it? If they do, do they follow through or are the merely paying lip service. Corporations are successful after obtaining complete integration from C-Suite down to managers and employees—and after they account for the culture of their customers. HR has been striving to set the direction for company strategy and be part of the solution, so this is our time. Take this information and engage your leadership with a case for inclusion (for example, the LGBT individuals average the most disposable income and 90 percent of their money is spent based on consumer preference—meaning they will switch brands to purchase something from businesses that are inclusive and diversified—illuminating that inclusion is, quite literally, serious business).

M—MENTOR the new generation of workers for the next couple of years, as the majority of the labor force will be comprised by Baby Boomers and Millennials. Our team, project, and workforces need to be comprised of all generations. Use face-to-face team-building and ice-breakers; keep yourself flexible and open to understand differences. We will often have experiences employees with older tribal knowledge working side by side with a younger generation that has grown up with modern technology. Just because we observe their difference does not mean we should assume that Baby Boomers, Traditionalists, or Generation X are not interested in mechanization or learning how it can make their jobs and lives easier.

My husband is the smartest person I know. What he lacks in college education, he more than compensates for with his life experience, common sense, and business acumen. He is the one that was with me every day and got me through eight years of undergraduate and graduate school. When I received my MBA, I awarded him his own honorary doctoral degree. Mentors can make great things possible for people; don't underestimate the effect you can have by playing this role for someone.

B — BREAK DOWN barriers to inclusion by promoting positive differences and finding common ground between people. This is never easy, and future HR will surely have to spend some of their time mediating relationship issues at work; after all the upcoming Digital Native's will be the most diverse generation in history, in most ways imaginable, yet bias and prejudice will persist. We may not always want to admit it, but despite our differences in culture, values, morals, ethics, life experiences and anything that has shaped who we are, we are still very similar in many ways. It is HR's job to open the lines of communication and act as the conduit that connects people, helps us understand our differences, and finds our best qualities in one another. Everyone wants to be treated fairly, and everyone wants to be successful; inclusion works to everyone's favor.

R — RECRUIT, train, and retain an inclusive workforce. Utilize data analytics to calculate retirement numbers and future labor numbers. Sit down with your managers to develop and write an accurate job description for each position, including its essential functions. Recruit for the top talent not for nepotism or "the person I know." Yes, this still happens in this day and age, but when an organization hires the top candidate that truly fits the company, the real diversity, quality of culture, retention, employee engagement, and profits all rise.

Train beyond basic compliance requirements; professional development has been found to increase the profitability of employees by 135 percent. Develop social media and company branding to open a pipeline of future talent. Communicate successes, employee accomplishments, social responsibility, and inclusion initiatives (to name a few) on numerous online media, potentially including a website, Facebook, LinkedIn, Twitter and others, enabling consistent brand recognition.

A — ALIGN the mission and purpose of your business with your strategic hiring. Once you develop the purpose of your business and understand future job opportunities within, then you can strategically hire. For example: can the job duties be performed from home or another area, or does the person need to observe specific office hours? Bring into discussion with your leaders matters like transparent hiring, promotions, and work flexibility for the positions you'll need to supply in the future.

C — CHANGE the corporate culture. The future's workforce believes that social responsibility and ethical conduct are more important than money, and they are willing to change or expand careers until they find the right company to work for. Turnover is costly; if you are always replacing employees, your profits plummet as more and more money is spent hiring, onboarding, and training new workers. There must be systemic culture change, including decentralized organizations and flexible benefits whenever possible, to curb these costs.

E — EDUCATE our children and grandchildren. It is everyone's responsibility to get into the classrooms, colleges, universities, communities, job fairs, veteran's groups, and multiple different diversity organizations to combat the future skill shortage. Allow people to understand our future business needs. Effective organizations are the ones teamed with colleges, universities, and Chambers of Commerce that develop courses and seminars on skills and abilities that workers and leaders will need to succeed in tomorrow's organizations. It starts with our children; we are the future role models who will teach children that they can succeed, that our little ladies can grow up to be engineers, scientists, doctors, mechanics, pilots if they want — or that our little gentlemen can be our future nurses, flight attendants, or executive assistants if they wish.

It is the decent, moral and ethical course to embrace inclusion of all individuals in the workforce, on our teams— and in our lives, in our neighborhoods, in other countries, in our global communities. Inclusion creates innovation, creative advantages, fresh perspective, improvements and eventually, increased profits. We, HR professionals, are the ones that must commit to push our CEOs, Presidents, Vice Presidents, Senior Management and Managers to be truly inclusive of all applicants and employees. Engage leadership and workers across the generations; break down barriers; recruit, train, and retain the best people you can find; align business mission and purpose with your daily work, and make it a mission to change the culture around you for the better and educate people in your daily life.

To be truly successful in a diversified business world, HR must continuously analyze their company's inclusion of employee gender, ethnic background, culture, lifestyles, and disabilities, recommending policy changes as needed to maintain a harmonious work atmosphere and positive customer relations.

ABOUT THE AUTHOR
Nichole Cobb
CEBS, SHRM-SCP, SPHR

Nichole Cobb, CEBS, SHRM-SCP, SPHR, MBA is a Human Resources professional and has presented HR topics at local SHRM chapter meetings. Nichole has over 25 years of experience encompassing federal contracting, federal government work, and service in the United States Air Force.

Jocelyn Davis

Building a Great Workplace

We all know that HR has come—in the parlance of the sixties—a long way, baby! HR has evolved from the Personnel Department of the past, focused only on transactions, into the Human Resources that supports managers of people (and an increasingly heavy compliance workload). Our next evolution for HR is to become a strategic partner in our organizations, and in so doing, to serve two separate functions: (A) compliance and administration and (B) organizational development.

HR is continually balancing the competing demands of managing labor costs and the ever-mounting challenge of creating great places to work. The inevitable demographic changes in the workforce caused by the retirement of the Baby Boomer generation, combined with the emergence of younger generations with different expectations of work, make it all the more important—strategically—for organizations to be great workplaces. The future is likely to be one where employees have a number of choices about where and how they work. And employers will have to compete not only on the professional opportunity, compensation, and benefits they provide, but also the quality of their workplace.

The good news for HR professionals and anyone who leads, manages, supervises, or works with people—and I think that's pretty much everybody—is that there is robust and accessible science supporting how we can collaboratively create and sustain great places to work in our organizations.

This chapter is to present a simple, unified theory about how to create a great place to work, along with providing some practical suggestions for you as an employee, supervisor, or manager to make a great workplace a reality. We believe that when you create a great workplace, individuals flourish and organizations thrive. We've been applying this theory and related applications in our consulting practice and have educated hundreds of graduate students in the engineering project management program at the University of Maryland in its use to increase project success rates.

So what do we tell our clients and students about great places to work?

Great places to work are identified regularly in local and national surveys, and here's what they have in common: **(A)** happy, healthy people **(B)** working in a supportive and challenging organizational environment **(C)** with management and co-workers they trust, **(D)** all while doing purposeful work which provides them opportunities to learn and grow.

Part of the challenge is remembering that everyone is responsible for contributing. This isn't just a feel-good objective. This is a do-good objective: great workplaces allow organizations to create and sustain an environment where people can do their best work consistently, thereby achieving the organization's larger objectives. This is true across sector and industry lines.

This bears emphasis: great places to work are not solely the responsibility of management. Rather, great places to work require that the individual employee, workgroups, management, and the entire organization take responsibility for and developing and sustaining their workplace into a great place to work. All too frequently, employees look to management alone to make everything happen, overlooking the many opportunities within their purview to contribute meaningfully.

Happy, Healthy People

Great places to work begin with happy, healthy people. Individuals need to take personal action to assure that they are physically, mentally, emotionally, and spiritually healthy. Maintaining supportive relationship networks, regular exercise, appropriate sleep, healthy nutrition, a sense of personal happiness, and a comfortable work-life balance are essential. In a book titled *The Power of Full Engagement*, Loehr and Schwartz offer a comprehensive model, assessment, and tools for being what they call corporate athletes, happy healthy people at work.

Managers and organizations have an important role to play in having happy, healthy people at work. Their contribution is to create a work environment—physical environment and culture—which supports employees. Flexible or alternative work schedules, wellness programs, stress management, encouragement of work-life balance, healthy workspaces (light, plants, ergonomically sound equipment, quiet spaces, group spaces, et cetera), nutritious food options—these are but a few of the supportive actions managers and organizations can take.

Work-life balance is challenging because very few of us are able to do everything we want. We recommend thinking of work-life balance as a quarterly plan designed to realize your life's "strategic goals." Remember that plans start with a mission statement; the first element of good work-life balance is a clear definition of what you want to accomplish, which necessitates making choices consistent with your priorities and your resources. For example, defining quarterly work-life goals realistically, allowing a bit of slack in your schedule for unexpected demands, will make the attainment of work-life balance more likely and will support planning conversations between management and staff.

Supportive and Motivating Environment

An organization must have a few key elements to create a great place to work: a pleasant physical environment, competent and trusted management and organization, routine constructive feedback, a balanced emotional tone, a sense of pride in the organization, and a clear purpose by contributing value to clients or stockholders at large.

Trust within an organization supports sustainable high performance: trust the people are competent, reliable, and caring. Trust is multidimensional. And, as with everything discussed in this chapter, it can be assessed and developed.

Feedback, both positive and negative, is key to a positive workplace. Each of us has a native desire to learn and grow; near-continuous feedback is required to do that. This feedback may be provided through attainment of interim milestones, ongoing multidirectional conversations, new and more challenging assignments, and the formal feedback process we're all accustomed to. In our consulting work, we see feedback as a grossly underutilized tool—not just the negative feedback which people don't like to provide, but also feedback which provides commendation.

A good workplace will enhance the motivations of the people who work in it. Of course, the most durable type motivation is internal—the type compelled towards personal autonomy, purpose, belonging, and mastery. It's important to recognize that good managers don't always motivate *per se*; rather, they provide an environment in which people can tap into their own motivation. Dan Pink, author of *Drive*, says it all in a short YouTube video which I've included at the end of the chapter. Helping managers to update their toolkit for motivating great work is supported by education on the theory of motivation, training on the application, and recognizing and rewarding great managerial performance.

For a long time, managers have suggested that we leave our emotions at home, that they have no place in the workplace, but research over the last decade, including the work of Barbara Fredrickson at UNC Chapel Hill, have reported that our emotions, both positive and negative, influence our work performance. (I recommend her book *Positivity*.) We all learned in high school biology that negative emotions such as fear, anger, disgust, and shame draw out our protective emotions—the "fight, flight, or freeze" response. This is true in the wild and in the workplace. These emotions have their purpose in the workplace—when teaching a new skill or when immediate compliance is needed. Too many managers, however, rely solely on negative emotions, which close our generative thinking capabilities, moving many of us to do what we're asked and little more.

Positive emotions, on the other hand, are not just the antidote to negative emotions. Positive emotions actually build psychological capital, preparing us to effectively respond to future challenges. Positive emotions support generative thinking; they help us expand our social networks, allowing us to work more effectively within diverse workgroups. Sustainable performance requires a net positive emotional experience. HR has the opportunity and obligation to help managers fully realize the benefits of positive emotions in the workplace.

Purpose motivates. HR can help managers and staff know, understand, and remain aligned with the "why" of the work they do every day—how what we do pleases our clients and stakeholders and positively impacts society at large. This is an important but often-overlooked conversation within organizations.

This is where you see true *employee engagement*. Employee engagement is highly correlated with increased levels of discretionary effort at work and favorable changes in key performance indicators. More recently, a number of groups have supplemented their employees' engagement with a number of new initiatives designed to improve the experience of work and organizational outcomes; these include wellness, flexible work schedules, alternative work schedules, telework, more generous leave policies, concierge services at work, play spaces at work, and more creative physical work environments (in some industries). These are all great additions to workplace management—but, again, are not alone sufficient to create a great workplace.

Developing Good Managers

Research by the Gallup Organization clearly indicates that people leave managers, not companies.

Growing great managers is essential to a positive workplace. We see three avenues for developing great managers. The first avenue assumes that to be a great manager—a manager of people at work—you need to really understand people. The understanding of others at work is really a fuller understanding of yourself. We believe that good management is grounded in knowing yourself in order to know others. The second avenue is to recognize that "technical expertise and tenure does not a great manager make." The third avenue requires that we change the way we compensate managers, that we consider both accomplishment and how it was attained in figuring their reward.

This suggest some changes for HR in creating positive workplaces.

Know yourself, know others. As people grow within a company, they need to learn first about themselves, their own technical expertise, and then about others and how to manage others well. Only people with these strong management skills will be able to sustain outstanding results. People early in their careers need to know themselves well: their personality, strengths, weaknesses, emotional style, personal motivations, values, conflict style, learning style, and more. This is essential to supplement their technical knowledge and to be and effective team members. There are readily available, empirically validated, and cost-effective self-assessments that we believe should become a fundamental element of early employee development.

Research shows that focusing on strengths and capitalizing on them is more effective than the traditional weakness correction model commonly used by managers. Weakness correction is really only appropriate when we're seeking compliance or to build a specific skill—like we all experienced in English Composition class. Research has found that working from our strengths (assuming we have the requisite skills) is more enjoyable, more productive, and more motivating, and thereby yields better results in the workplace.

There are a number of strengths assessments available; the Gallup Organization's StrengthsFinder Assessment is one well-known assessment.

There are two other strengths assessments which we believe have significant merit. The first is the Values in Action Inventory of Character Strengths and Virtues developed by Chris Peterson and Martin E. P. Seligman. (This self-assessment is available free at the University of Pennsylvania's positive psychology website.) These strengths describe who you are, not what you do.

The second strengths self-assessment is the Realise2 developed by Alex Linley at the Center for Applied Positive Psychology in the U.K. This strengths assessment focuses on you at work, with attention to three elements: your specific strength, how often you use it, and how energizing the use of this strength is. Linley's tool allows individuals and teams to look at their portfolio of strengths, assess how they currently use them, and determine how they might allocate them differently to obtain best results. This is our favorite, and we have used it successfully to coach individuals and teams to higher levels of performance.

Management as a distinct expertise. In our consulting work, we are often asked to resolve difficult, sometimes toxic, team dynamics. With few exceptions, these situations have arisen because people—often very good people—were promoted to manager based on tenure or technical expertise, but lacked the interest and knowledge necessary to be a great manager. We believe that HR can support creating positive workplaces by clearly articulating a philosophy of management as a discrete area of expertise, one that needs to be developed alongside goal expertise and experience so that, when someone is promoted to management, they are not the foot of that learning curve. This can be accomplished by developmental assignments, education, shadowing more experienced managers, and a clear articulation of a philosophy that holds good management as essential to the organization's success.

Recognize and reward the *what* and the *how*. Managers of operating divisions find the growing number of HR initiatives dizzying when trying to balance core work execution with HR management responsibilities. And since they are rewarded for the *what,* but not *how,* managers focus on measurable results and not the quality of the workplace they create.

In a recent conversation with a senior project manager at another company, we talked about the need for great places to work, and particularly about how detrimental chronic stress can be to employee health, well-being, and performance. He saw it and he agreed, but his position was very clear: as a project manager, he had short- to intermediate-term deliverables defined by a specific project scope, schedule, and budget, and his performance evaluation and performance bonus were based upon them. He admitted that he was managing the project to earn his performance bonus, even though it was creating unhealthy stress levels for his team members; any burnout that they experienced would be some other project manager's problem when they moved to their next project. *Not his problem.* His incentives were clear—but his answer would undoubtedly have been different had there been a fourth deliverable on his project, one related to creating and sustaining a great place to work.

Call to Action

The so-called "soft skills" of HR are the new hard skills for the workplace of the future if we want to create positive workplaces. Organizations who fail to create positive workplaces will be unlikely to be able to attract and retain the people they need to succeed..

In rethinking HR, we need to take some action:

- Unified theory of what creates a great place to work
- Early professional development efforts focusing on growing the individual as a person and not simply as a technical expert
- Recognizing management as a separate technical expertise and beginning training early (and in parallel with technical expertise development)

- Redesigning reward and recognition systems to address not only the *what* of the work, but the *how* of the work, so that people at work are not depreciable assets
- Involving everyone, not just management, in responsibility to create and sustain a positive workplace.

We know from our consulting and teaching experience that these are profound changes which will help us create and sustain great places to work.

Developing the best places—and from those places, the best people—to work in our companies can be difficult. Just remember that a great workplace isn't only the wish of Human Resources or your leaders, but everyone's wish. It isn't just a fresh coat of paint, but it's changing a place to impact on how people perform—and therefore how your organization performs.

It's not just about feeling good. It's about doing good.

Quick References

Nelson Hart/Happiness at Work Assessment:
> https://nelsonhart.happinessatworksurvey.com/try

Dan Pink on Motivation:
> https://www.youtube.com/watch?v=u6XAPnuFjJc.

Jocelyn Davis

Jocelyn S. Davis is a management consultant, coach, and educator with expertise in helping individuals and organizations (corporate, government, and non-profit) improve their effectiveness. She brings a unique blend of financial, operational, goverance, and organizational development experience to her work. She is widely recognized for her expertise in applying the principles of Positive Psychology to creating a great place to work.

Ms. Davis is the founder of Nelson Hart LLC, a professional services firm which provides consulting and educational services to organizations: strategic planning, governance, organizational development, leadership, and executive coaching. She helps leaders and managers invest the time to know themselves: their strengths and their lesser sttengths, their interests, and their passions using principles of positive psychology championed by Dr. Martin Seligman of the University of Pennsylvania, the Gallup Organization, and many others in the field.

Ms. Davis is an adjunct instructor at the University of Maryland, Clark School of Engineering Project Management Center for Excellence, where she teaches *Managing Project Teams* and *The Evolving Project Leader*. She presents on the topic of positive psychology—flourishing individuals yielding thriving organizations—to audiences globally.

She has previously been published in the *Oxford University Handbook of Positive Psychology and Work* (edited by Linley and Harrington, published in 2013) and in the *Gower Handbook of People in Projects* (edited by Lock and Scott, published in 2013). Her contributions to anthologies have focused on the education of technical managers to become outstanding leaders of people.

Ms. Davis is a graduate of the College of William and Mary in Williamsburg, Virginia. She practiced for many years as a certified public accountant.

Kristin Dunlevy

Financial Wellness @ Work

"Given that financial stress is a (if not the) leading cause of stress, most experts anticipate financial wellness programs will be core part of most employee benefit packages within next 3-5 years."

—Personal Financial Employee Education Foundation—

Ready for a rude awakening? 77% of Americans live paycheck-to-paycheck—and that severe financial stress costs employers (on average) $2,000 per employee per year, according to the Personal Finance Employee Education Foundation.

I have been a retirement plan consultant for 20 years. I often explain to my colleagues that, when we only encourage employees to pursue long-term financial goals without giving attention to present-day financial wellness, we're putting the cart in front of the horse. That is: we encourage employees to contribute significantly to their 401(k) accounts without addressing foundations of good money management, like maintaining an adequate balance in checking and savings accounts, following plans to reduce or eliminate debt, and sticking to a monthly budget.

Until we address financial basics, we will always fall short in properly preparing people for a successful retirement. For that reason, this chapter does not focus on retirement savings, 401(k)s, or the other popular benefits discussions in HR—instead, it focuses on financial wellness, its foundations, and why it makes a difference to Human Resources and to the organizations we serve.

Poor financial knowledge, attitudes, and behaviors are pervasive problems in the US workforce. Consider the following data compiled in "Financial Literacy Pays Dividends," a white paper by Financial Fitness Group:

- 77% of Americans live paycheck-to-paycheck.
- 56% of American adults don't have a budget.
- 41% of Americans grade themselves as a C, D, or F in personal finance.
- 40% carry credit card debt month-to-month.
- 32% have no non-retirement savings.
- 29% can handle emergencies only by using a credit card.
- 28% don't pay their bills on time.
- 22% don't know how much they spend on food, housing, and entertainment.
- 21% believe that winning the lottery is the most viable way to fund retirement.

In turn, 80 percent or more of employees—over 100 million people in the United States—suffer from moderate to high financial stress, according to Financial Fitness Group.

Research suggests that financial stress costs employers an average of $1,140 per employee per year through turnover, absenteeism, payroll expenses, and healthcare. In total, financial stress could cost US employers more than $150 billion per year in lost profits and productivity.

It is estimated that financial illiteracy costs organizations more than $1 million in lost profits and productivity for every 1,000 employees. And it can affect more than just the entry-level or support positions; financial stress plagues top earners as well as rank-and-file employees, as often nowadays they can be burdened with significant debts.

Furthermore, financial stress can be the largest obstacle for your company's physical wellness program, as these stresses commonly lead to certain unhealthy behaviors such as smoking, weight gain, and alcohol or drug abuse according to the American Psychological Association. A survey by the Associated Press and AOL shows Americans with significant debt also suffer more health problems, including higher rates of depression, high blood pressure, heart attacks, back pain, migraines, ulcers, and insomnia.

In other words: financial stress has real, painful, and permanent consequences that could be (and probably are) affecting people all over your organization. Yet when Human Resources thinks and talks about financial well-being, they usually aren't thinking and talking about the everyday financial challenges people face.

Unfortunately, the reach of financial stress extends beyond our wallets and our arteries; it can affect all aspects of our lives, including our personal and intimate relationships.

> *"A couple with $10,000 in debt and no savings is twice as likely to divorce as a couple with no debt and $10,000 in savings."*
> —CNN—

The good news is that foundational finance goals are often simpler, and the first one is no exception: maintain an adequate balance in your savings account. This has been shown to reduce financial stress materially and should be the first financial goal of a financial wellness program.

Most employers are aware of the personal consequences; according to a 2015 AON Hewitt survey, 93% of employers plan to add or improve a basic financial wellness program to their development initiatives in the next 12 months.

However, we need to rethink how we deliver these financial wellness programs, as past programs have not been as effective as people hoped. Employers spend over $2 billion annually on employee benefit communications, but with very few meaningful or measurable results. For example, I have a new client that offers (expensive) quarterly employee education workshops. Over the past six years, their best attendance rate is a little over 2% each quarter, and less than 9% of their employee base attends the workshops. This is not effective and I believe it cannot continue.

"If you want something you've never had, you must be willing
to do something you've never done."

—Thomas Jefferson—

We can have financially sounder employees through programs that cover the basics:

- Savings
- Debt Reduction
- Budgets
- Employee Benefits/Insurance
- Retirement Savings
- Giving

However, the program can amplify the results if it embraces education, psychology, and our competitive spirit. An effective and scalable approach could be as simple as:

Assess—Educate—Inspire—Reward—Reassess

Wellness assessments are nothing new for employers. According to research conducted by Wisconsin University professor, Dr. John Hoffmire, employers spend $7 billion annually on Health Risk Assessments to help the corporate wellness programs improve physical fitness. Fortunately, Financial Risk Assessments are easier and more cost-effective.

◆　◆　◆　◆　◆

ASSESS—EDUCATE—INSPIRE—REWARD—REASSESS

"Real knowledge is to know the extent of one's ignorance."
—Confucius—

A quick survey of a few simple questions and emotional evaluation can assess your workforces' overall financial stress level.

A sample of these questions could include:

- How many weeks of take home pay do you (and your spouse) have in an easily accessible savings account(s)?
- How much non-mortgage debt do you (and your spouse) have?
- How many open credit card accounts do you (and your spouse) have?
- Do you have and adhere to a monthly budget?
- On a scale from 1-10, rate how anxious you are about your personal finances with 1 being no anxiety and 10 being extremely anxious.

Once you become aware of the level of financial stress your workforce is experiencing, you have learned something important about them—and even having read this chapter, you might be surprised at what you find.

◆　◆　◆　◆　◆

ASSESS—**EDUCATE**—INSPIRE—REWARD—REASSESS

"Education is the most powerful weapon which you can use to change the world."
—Nelson Mandela—

You need an independent financial education program that aligns with the needs and resources of employees. There are many financial education programs to consider and more emerging to meet this growing demand. The Personal Finance Employee Education Foundation lists some quality providers on its website (www.pfeef.org), but here are a few providers that you may want to explore:

- LearnVest
- SmartDollar
- Financial Center
- Forum Credit Union
- Elements Financial

- Financial Finesse
- FinFit
- HelloWallet
- BeManaged
- Financial Fitness Group

When considering what might fit your organization best, assess the programs' delivery method, technology features, behavior modification, reporting, conflicts of interest, and payment method.

Although education is a necessary component of an effective program, personal finance is 20% head knowledge and 80% behavior. Remember that your program must inspire a change in behavior.

◆   ◆   ◆   ◆   ◆

ASSESS — EDUCATE — **INSPIRE** — REWARD — REASSESS

"Nothing is impossible; the word itself says 'I'm possible'!"
—Audrey Hepburn—

A truly motivational program can be incorporated into your corporate culture. One firm painted the core values on the walls of their conference rooms. Instead of the conference rooms being named after the founders of the company or a letter of the alphabet, each room had a name that corresponded with a core value of the organization. This was a constant source of inspiration for their workforce. This is an example of a repetitive lifecycle to have long-term and permanent results for the workforce. A good financial wellness program provider can help develop a fun, inspirational, and motivational campaign that can champion your corporate culture.

Again, we can begin to reduce our level of stress by simply starting and maintaining a small savings account. A savings account application could be included in the onboarding process for new employees. As a matter of fact, an automatic 10% deposit of net pay with the right to opt- out could be effective. This could inspire good financial habits.

◆   ◆   ◆   ◆   ◆

ASSESS — EDUCATE — INSPIRE — **REWARD** — REASSESS

"Recognition is not a scarce resource.
You can't use it up or run out of it."
—Susan M. Heathfield—

Think of a Fitbit that continually monitors, reminds, and reports our physical progress and lets us share and recognize our accomplishments with our friends. The "Financial Fitbit" concept can provide virtual rewards, constant support, and the motivation we need to achieve our financial goals. Some creative and affordable ideas include free merchandise from local businesses, free jeans day, time off, and gift cards.

Reward is what keeps the cycle of growth and improvement turning—so be sure that your financial wellness program provides ways of monitoring and reminding about financial goals, but also, that it provides a way of connecting your employees together and recognizing personal improvements.

◆　◆　◆　◆　◆

ASSESS — EDUCATE — INSPIRE — REWARD — **REASSESS**

"Diagnosis is not the end, but the beginning of practice."
—Martin H. Fischer—

Reassessing your employees' financial stress level after your financial fitness program will tell you if it is worthy of being included in the corporate annual budget. Let the results tell the truth.

For now, the good news is that the results of a financial wellness program in the workplace can be phenomenal, based on a five-year research project conducted by Financial Fitness Group and Wisconsin University (which covered 700 employers, more than 100,000 employees, and 400,000 hours of education):

1,000 EE Base	Financial Stress Estimated Lost Profits		
	Extreme Stress	**Moderate Stress**	**Low Stress**
Per Employee	$2,000	$750	$0
1st Assessment— Before FFG	33%	48%	19%
2nd Assessment— After FFG	22%	53%	25%
Reduction to Profits (Before)	-$660,000	-$360,000	$0
Reduction to Profits (After)	-$440,000	-$397,500	$0

The average improvement was estimated to be $182,500 per year for every 1,000 workers. This doesn't even take into account all of the benefit that employees and their families receive that doesn't appear in the company's numbers, much less all of the stress it relieves and happiness it creates. Especially knowing that over three quarters of Americans live paycheck-to-paycheck, do you still feel like discussing 401(k)s with employees?

A short ten years ago, far fewer employers had health wellness programs; now they're commonplace. Financial wellness programs are that next need; larger employers are more aware of these issues and many are already seeking solutions. I expect that, ten years from now, most employers will have a financial fitness program for its substantial and recurring impacts on profit, culture, stability and community.

ABOUT THE AUTHOR
Kristin Dunlevy
QPFC, AIF®

Kristin V. Dunlevy, QPFC, AIF®, joined Pro-Course Fiduciary Advisors, LLC with over 25 years of broad industry experience through her work for a certified public accounting firm, an actuarial firm, and registered investment advisory firms. As a specialist in 401(k), 403(b), 457 and other institutional retirement plans, Kristin provides plan sponsors with relatable communication, foresight, and customized solutions. Her leadership and industry knowledge of investment management, asset allocation, market strategy, fee and expense benchmarking, service provider searches, and retirement plan design enables her to fulfill her passion to make retirement plans more effective and align with plan sponsor's overall objectives. Her passion empowers plan sponsor's number one asset—their employees—to reach financial wellness and a financially successful retirement.

Throughout her career, Kristin has served as an investment fiduciary in her roles as a president, principal, managing director, director of research, investment officer, manager, and advisor. Kristin is a published author and has been quoted in local and international publications such as Louisville Business First and London's Financial Times. She serves on the Louisville Employee Benefits Council Executive Committee and currently serves as LEBC's President. She also serves on the American Society of Pension Professionals & Actuaries' Government Affairs Committee.

She earned her Bachelor of Science in Mathematics with Magna Cum Laude from the University of Louisville. She resides in Louisville, Kentucky with her husband and two of their five children.

*Accredited Investment Fiduciary (AIF®) designation

JC Gibson

Shhh! You Might Be Doing OD!
OD Philosophy and Practice in the Workplace

I practice Organizational Development (OD) every day, but I never, ever use those words (or letters). When OD techniques are applied correctly, it should seem to others like common sense.

Even though I have a degree specifically in this field—a Master's in Organizational Development from Case Western Reserve—I always resist placing labels or limits on what an OD role could be in an organization. There is no one tool we always use, no single process that works for every organization, every time, or for every developmental phase of a company's life. As with being a physician or an attorney, you apply what you know from real career experience to the matter at hand; if you work hard and have a little bit of luck, you learn from each new situation in a way that makes you better as a practitioner. That's why I'm always looking for both structured and un-structured ways to hone my professional skills.

It is my main operating principle that **Organizational Development must be woven into the fabric of an organization or it will not be able to change culture.**

For this reason, I most often say I'm an HR generalist with a bag of specialist tools; I support executive staffs in growing companies. To do my job well, I focus on using the right tool for the right job at the right time. But I've found that even if you have the best toolkit possible—the latest assessments and process maps, the newest readings, access to good peers and the leadership—the success of Organizational Development is still a function of how well your team can absorb difficulties, learn from them, and use the tools and methodologies available to elevate performance behavior beyond the employees' expectations.

In some ways, my role in the organization is to be one of the leaders just out of sight who helps others improve and, therefore, helps the whole ensemble improve. My senior HR role should be to influence the CEO and executive group to speed up, to slow down to consider certain options, or to swerve and avoid collisions. The "OD hat" comes out to add structure to that internal counsel; I reach into my toolkit and produce whatever is needed help the executive group stay on the road, stay focused, and keep their pedal to the metal.

Again, organizational improvement comes when you apply the right tools with the right people at the right time. Arriving in an organization and dumping out your toolkit, however stocked it may be, does no one any good. Even with great OD tools and stories of success from past companies, you may find them falling on deaf ears if the organization isn't ready for change. Sometimes, facilitating change is forcing change; I've driven organizations in both manners.

The best OD/HR practitioner is one who can get the immediate tasks aligned and completed while enthusiastically listening to the organization to help it move faster, with less friction and with more clarity in its direction. Listen, and then act. Then, model to other executives how to "listen and then act."

Even the best pro baseball players couldn't hit a fastball at two years old. They have to be developmentally ready, aware of the goal, and mentally mature enough to make the right decisions in the heat of the game. Yet, in the opposite direction, all of the best baseball players were once two years old; they just needed the right exposure and practice. Solid OD/HR staff develop both the tools and the timing for employees to make big hits in the organization.

Let's be clear, if it isn't already: an OD/HR practitioner is not a passive role. It means always pushing, probing, cajoling, teaching, leading and—many times—pushing some more. Like giving birth (or so I hear), this process is built around pushing, it's never easy, and never seems to end.

Traditional HR starts with making sure that the "trains run on time"—building up the competence and credibility to be seen as a resource for the organization. But to use another transport analogy, you have to consider your contributions somewhat more as "fixing the bus as it's driving down the road." Eventually, the improvements (and your skill at making them, even during motion) should have transformed the bus into something else entirely, perhaps a plane with a bus-shaped cabin. This is considerably harder than simply "making sure the trains run on time"—it requires you to always be a leader, to always think in these terms whether you're leading from backstage or the spotlight.

In my experience, it isn't complicated to help organizations fix themselves by integrating Organizational Development values and techniques into the everyday habits of the company. Especially rewarding, the fixes accelerate when you begin to create improvements to which the employees and stockholders have said it's about time. The following are some of the OD principles I've applied as a CHRO in past companies, roughly following the employee life cycle in any company.

Hiring

- Hire for greatness. Know and articulate what you want. Buy or develop testing that gives everyone a head start in eliminating candidates.
- Tired but true: 'A' people hire 'A' candidates, 'B' people hire 'C' candidates. Use your best people to be active in the recruitment for key positions. I've been successful, in both private equity and in multi-national public companies, at putting hiring processes in place to build consensus about an executive profile (using 'A' people) and then finding an executive with the best fit (another 'A' person).
- A well-written job description is a good start, but having a practical scoring sheet for assessing a candidate interview will bring it all home when the selection discussion occurs.

Fast Starts For Fast Cars

- There has to be some orientation time for new employees, but as quickly as possible, put people in roles and projects that will have immediate, impactful, and visible results on the company. The new hires will pick up the pace for everyone around them and they will build their own network with only a little help. You don't need to teach a racehorse to run; just put it in the race and let it run. The other horses will run, too.

- Tell people they are great, but occasionally—they don't need constant back-patting, and they realize the goals have been achieved with their help when the company "wins" at the end of the budget year. This is a simple Organizational Development principle that changes the culture of the company to recognize performance—and to expect it from everyone.

Compensation

- The second chapter of an Econ 101 textbook will tell you that incentives drive behavior, and this is mostly true. But the second chapter of a Psych 101 textbook will help us get specific: in studying human behavior, psychologists have found that intermittent rewards drive much more sustained effort than other rewards. To convert this concept into reality, I design and communicate the appropriate incentive plans to each respective level of the organization and, for their plan, have people sign off on it every year. It's like a marriage vow renewal—except you can change the terms of the deal!
- Make sure you reward high performers with intermittent incentives in addition to the regular incentive plans. It could be a little bonus money; it could be dinner with the CEO; it might be the next big organizational challenge for which they could lead a project. Don't let high performers get bored. Create lots of C-suite interaction and appropriate kinds of pressure that stretches them.

Training

- OD is best when it is focused on planting the right seeds in the right spots. When "how" you do it becomes as important as "what" gets done, the culture of an organization begins to evolve.
- Training is a lever to move and change the organization. To change the organization, the training has to change the employee. For this reason, invest only in what makes the employee better on a daily basis (and what is needed for compliance).
- For managers, invest in practical supervision and teambuilding skills.
- Always attach training to a formal process. Consider giving program participants a spotlight with a short senior management presentation. Build a platform where

the employee can brag about the impact they've made and let them know that you are interested in hearing what they've learned.

Performance Management and Evaluation

- Roles only exist to support the organization in achieving its ultimate goal, which is the service of the customer. I'm a strong believer that every employee either supports the customer directly or supports the person supporting the customer.
- If possible, automate the process. No one likes writing (or reading and scoring) evaluations. Work hard on setting up the goals first and let the evaluation create itself from them. Wherever possible, tie everyone's personal goals and values to the company's goals and values. I've introduced values and objectives to the evaluation process, and it has completely changed the tone of the conversation with employees.
- When "how" you do it becomes as important as "what" gets done, the culture of an organization begins to evolve. **Teaching that the thought process and conversation should start with <u>what you appreciate</u> leads to the feeling of recognition that money can't buy.**

Corrective Action and Termination

- There should never be a surprise in a case of ordinary termination. However, just about everyone needs a midcourse correction every once in a while. Be clear and be quick when you realize that a correction is needed. The confrontation can be emotional, but if it is forthright, it can help fix minor behaviors.
- If behaviors don't change in a reasonable amount of time, don't wait around — execute the termination. The change is almost always for the best and the replacement process is usually a healthy exercise (see "hiring for greatness" above).

Team Development

- Everyone says the words, but very few hear themselves say them. If a team is expected to deliver high-performing results, they will need time to practice being a team. It doesn't take much time, effort, or fertilizer, yet the results can be staggeringly good.

- This is probably the part of OD that is the most visible in organizations through activities such as testing, practice scenarios, and forcing the articulation of group rules so everyone is on the same page. We make these efforts because, again, it takes time for a team to learn working together; basketball players spend a long time playing together before they can make passes without looking. Remember, too, that just as the team has to show up and practice, each individual has to give their time and attention to being a full-time player if they're going to belong to a high-performing team.

Engagement Surveys
- A well-done survey can become a road map for the company's culture. Take them seriously.
- Anonymous surveys are critical in delivering wake-up calls to organizations. However, unless you are going to communicate and act upon on the results of the surveys in a timely manner, don't waste your time.
- Internal customer surveys allow another level of feedback that produces real and immediate information. A skillful OD/HR practitioner should be able to leverage this to push rapid organizational change.

High Potentials and Succession Planning
HiPos are always in the succession-planning book, but you don't need HiPos to see the benefits of even a simple succession plan. It should be a CEO Direct Report's performance requirement to present a two-level succession plan every year and update it as needed. Even if it is a tactical plan of who would take the role if a colleague resigned tomorrow, the act of defining this plan removes confusion from the decisions about what types of people to hire, who to train, and who should be retained or retired.

A final question some of you may think to ask: internal or external OD consultants? The answer is "yes," as there's a time and place for each.

Organizational Development isn't just for outside experts or your company's C-suite; it's for Human Resources, it's for managers, and it's for all employees who are ready to be serious for the company. Begin by being the leader, by being serious and showing people, in practice, how these principles make a difference on working culture. Then, day by day, you only have to use the right tool at the right time for the right person.

JC Gibson

JC Gibson joined Firstsource as Executive Vice President of North American Human Resources in 2013, bringing more than 20 years of Human Resources experience to his role. Most recently, he was with the private equity group Welsh, Carson, Anderson and Stowe, where he was the senior HR leader for portfolio companies such as MedE America/WebMD and S.H.P.S. Prior to that, Mr. Gibson was Global Director at Ferro Corporation, serving 5,000 employees across 20 countries. He is a graduate of Case Western Reserve University with a Master's Degree in Organizational Development and Analysis.

Sherri Harbsmeier

Moving Your Company to Great Heights

My journey of employee engagement began in March of 2000. I was approached by the CEO of a local organization, and he asked me: would I consider taking a Human Resources leadership role supporting more than 400 employees? I'd be overseeing employees in Louisville, Kentucky and Bedford, Texas, in an area of the company known as Central Patient Account Services (CPAS)—something all too familiar to me from my earlier days at Humana. This part of the organization was considered, from a Human Resources perspective, one of the worst areas to support.

I remember going to the interview and beginning to size things up. I remember noticing that the walls were painted battleship gray in the call center. Then I met with the new CEO, who told me that turnover in this division was at 167%, manager ratios were at 100:1, wages weren't competitive to attract the right candidates, the quality of recent hires hadn't been the best—and the list went on.

At that time, I was working as a Human Resources Manager with the Humana Military Healthcare division, where I started at its infancy and was quite proud of the accomplishments and reputation we had earned. All Humana employees wanted to transfer to that part of the organization. It was a fun and rewarding place to be! But I knew there were no growth opportunities in Human Resources; I was ready for a new challenge, and my immediate Director encouraged me to take this opportunity.

So, on July 24, 2000, I joined HCA Healthcare and embarked on a new journey, and a challenging one both personally and professionally. From the beginning, I had to question whether I'd made the right career decision. I wasn't so sure especially after the first day of work, when a Director of Operations told me there was a drug deal happening between two employees on the fourth floor stairwell—and what was I going to do about it? Nothing like calling the police and firing two employees on your first day. What had I gotten myself into? Were we, as a management team, able to overcome these types of problems?

I was one of three new directors and part of a total team of six who came onboard to help support and re-engineer what was known as Central Patient Collections, renamed National Patient Account Services (NPAS). The end result of our collaborative efforts was to become one of the best self-pay collections organizations in the industry and provide top-rated customer service. How did we get there?

In broad terms first: the organization worked with an outside consulting company who provided recommendations to be implemented within the center. As department heads, we worked with our respective teams and implemented the initiatives that made most sense for our resources and needs. We also worked through cross-functional teams on various projects suggested by the consulting group.

The Human Resources team implemented the following improvements immediately:

1. Wages—approval to recruit candidates at a higher wage in order to attract more qualified applicants. All current staff wages were adjusted.
2. Recruitment Resources—reviewed past recruitment resources and focused efforts on identifying better sources in the community and media.
3. Pre-employment testing—worked with a team of psychologists and developed testing based on approved competencies and metrics. The individual test results were compared to performance in order to understand the reliability of the testing.
4. Behavioral Interviewing questions—identified competencies relevant to the collections position and developed interview questions to identify the most-qualified applicants. Identified additional attributes instrumental to the position with the Operational Directors and management team.
5. Background checks—the organization was not conducting appropriate background checks on employees. Criminal checks were completed locally and nationally along with pre-employment drug testing.
6. New Employee Orientation—the orientation process was standardized so all new employees were hearing consistent information. Human Resources policies and

procedures were reviewed with leadership and the management team and appropriate changes were made in line with the company's new vision and values philosophy.

From 2000 to 2006, we continued to refine departmental processes, participated in the organization's yearly employee engagement surveys, created action plans, and acted to improve overall engagement and performance metrics. Our hourly and management team members were all contributors to this!

In spring of 2006, I was invited by an officer of the Louisville Society for Human Resource Management to attend a Best Places to Work in Kentucky (BPTW) awards dinner. She knew I had been working with my management team to improve engagement within my team, and she felt it may be time to consider applying for the award to be appropriately recognized within the community. I immediately started discussing the application process with my executive team.

In fall of 2006, we completed the application process to get NPAS on the list with some of the best employers in the state. The news came in January 2007: we made the list of Best Places to Work in Kentucky! Needless to say, that was a very exciting time for us as an organization; all of the hard work by employees, managers, department heads, and our executive team had finally paid off. More than forty of us traveled to Frankfort, the state capital, to hear our name recognized for the first time as the 18th Best Place to Work Winner (out of 25) in the Large Company Category. Especially as a collections organization, we were ecstatic about this ranking!

Our employees' job roles remain very challenging to this day. They speak to patients who may be unemployed, dying of cancer, and have no way to pay their bill. It takes the right spirit to do this job each day. They have to be compassionate, but forceful enough to make something work within the system. It's a hard job. But NPAS has returned to the list of Best Places to Work for nine years—the Texas office, too, has been recognized as a Best Place to Work in Texas six times. If our employees can do their jobs well and rate their workplaces this highly, something here must be working. So let's break it down.

The chart on the following page shows how the dollars collected increased per FTE for the period of 2003 through 2009 as our employee engagement scores increased.

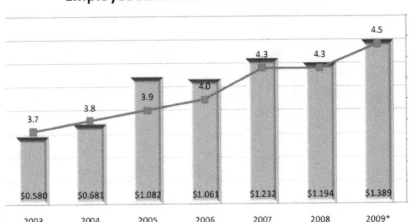

Employee Satisfaction and Performance

Whether you are a start-up organization or going through a re-engineering process, the following components must be part of your employee engagement strategy in order to move your performance metrics upward:

Executive Support
The executive team has to live and breathe employee engagement and speak to this topic continuously with their direct reports and all employees. This has to become part of the everyday culture.

The Right Survey Administrator
During my tenure at HCA Healthcare, we had two different survey administrators. The surveys were very similar—both had "Q12 questions" (The Gallup 12 Index) and the ability to customize additional questions and create ad hoc reports for you.

Consider: how does the survey administrator identify employees who take the survey? Will the employees understand that their information is confidential and they will not be singled out for items stated in the survey? (This tends to be a common concern voiced.) Lastly, how exactly will they report the data? The reporting format is just as important as the questions asked. If you are not able to retrieve your data in a useful manner, the survey is not going to be valuable to you.

Educating Employees About the Survey Process

All employees need to understand the importance and meaning of the survey tool being administered. They need to know that you, as a management team, will listen to the feedback, act seriously upon what is voiced, and be honest if there are items you cannot address and the reasons why. The survey is for all employees regardless of their position. All voices are heard—that's its job!

Remember: the worst thing to do as an organization is to not do anything. This will kill your efforts in a heartbeat, and the trust will take a long time to recover.

High Participation Rates

Employees have to understand that, without their voice, there can be no change in their favor. High participation rates are crucial to the success of an organization's results. As an idea, use posters to show the participation rate at the beginning and end of the week. Give incentives at the end of the survey period for reaching a particular goal, such as dress down days, pizza parties, or some other form of appreciation your employees would enjoy.

Process Improvement

Within our environment, we have been successful having different forums where employees have a voice, feel valued and appreciated, and have an impact on the ways things are performed.

Employee Task Force or Employee Activities Group

This group consists of employees from various departments within the center, both hourly and salaried. They meet monthly, or as often as needed, to discuss relevant topics including but not limited to:

- Resources needed to do their jobs, technology
- How employees are recognized and appreciated in the work environment
- The way work is completed and could be done better
- Communications and how they can be improved so that everyone always has the same information
- Professional Development opportunities available in the center

- Additional benefits employees would like to see in the workplace
- Conveniences and creature comforts, such as food in the vending machines

Topics such as wages—sticky as they are—should be directed to Human Resources for review.

Ad Hoc Teams

These are groups of employees brought together for a specific objective because of their expertise and knowledge. By their nature, there are no typical *ad hoc* teams you should expect to need; just know you have the option to form them.

Known Results

Employees at all levels need to be reminded what has already been accomplished as a result of their voice. The more you communicate about what has been addressed, the more constructive and enthusiastic the thoughts that the organization will hear. You can disseminate this information via emails, posters throughout the workplace, newsletters, blogs, and any media forums popularly used in your location.

Reporting and Communication

There are the standard reports the administrator creates for the organization around the following types of topics—Leadership, Staffing, Voice, Rewards, Culture, Quality, and Outcomes. Various administrators may call these by different names. Within our organization, we think all the way down to the managerial level to give each team their specific information to begin improvement. Managers are expected to create action plans around their opportunities for improvement. These are discussed regularly and part of our managerial overall incentives.

To earn employee engagement, there is a lot of work on the ground floor—but once you incorporate some of your new activities into a daily routine, it becomes habit. We are proud to have some of the highest engagement scores in the organization. Running (or working in) a collection agency is not an easy job, and it does require something of its people. But it all goes to show that, regardless of the job you're there to do, there is always potential for your employees to be happy, highly engaged, and performing at their best!

ABOUT THE AUTHOR

Sherri Harbsmeier

SPHR, SHRM-SCP

Sherri L. Harbsmeier, SPHR, SHRM-SCP, is the Regional Director of Human Resources of Revenue Cycle Point Solutions, a subsidiary of Parallon and HCA Healthcare. She brings more than 25 years as an HR professional and business partner in the healthcare industry in the areas of strategic planning, recruitment, employee retention, work/life balance programs, employee relations, and benefits. She has worked in start-up organizations and assisted in the re-engineering of current environments for the past twenty years along with having these work environments be recognized as Best Places to Work cultures in TX and KY for the past nine years.

Sherri has been a member of the National Society for Human Resources Management and Louisville SHRM since 1997 and has held a variety of volunteer roles in the local chapter. Sherri holds a Bachelor's Degree in Human Resources from the University of Louisville.

She resides in Louisville with her husband Bryan, daughter Alexis, son Nick, cats Cali and Dottie, and her dog London.

Michele Fantt Harris

Taking the Challenge for Employee Well-Being

At National Cooperative Bank, we had a problem. Our healthcare costs had been rising every year, and suddenly our annual premium increase was hitting the double digits! We had tried to keep our annual medical premium rate increase below 10%—but now we were afraid that future increases would escalate, and as a small employer our options were limited. Changing to cheaper health plans with higher deductibles and co-pays wasn't desirable to us because it would place a greater burden on the Bank's 400 employees. So, the CEO charged Human Resources with developing an innovative solution to this problem.

In this chapter, I'll be outlining what our team did and how we came together to solve this problem—and, in sharing how we've grown and improved personally and professionally within National Cooperative Bank (NCB), I've included some recommendations for addressing healthcare concerns at work and taking a proactive approach to mitigating those problems.

To get started, NCB's HR team researched the root cause of the rising healthcare costs. The higher-than-average claims for medical services and prescriptions owed largely to chronic health problems attributable to lifestyle. Unhealthy behaviors among workers cost employers an average of $670 per employee annually, according to the 2011 Thomson Reuters Workforce Wellness Index. Fortunately, lifestyle problems, while persistent, can be altered or corrected.

Evidence indicates that healthier lifestyles among employees can be beneficial to the workplace in some of the following ways:

- Employees who pursue healthful behaviors have fewer illnesses and injuries, and they recover from illness and injuries faster.
- Employees who participate in regular physical activity have increased cardiovascular endurance and reduced risk of cardiovascular disease.
- Those who adhere to low-fat diets, refrain from smoking, avoid excessive use of alcohol, and get enough sleep are often adding literal years to their lives.

Employees who do all of the above are more alert, more positive in their outlook, and better able to deal with the stresses and constant changes of today's world.

The HR team decided that our solution would have to include ways to improve the overall health of NCB employees through healthier lifestyle choices, such as improved diet and more exercise. The overall goal of the Bank's health program was to reduce our annual totals of medical and prescription claims, and to have a healthier and more productive workforce besides. We established four objectives for the program:

1. To make employees aware of the need to improve their health,
2. To offer employees effective weight loss and management strategies,
3. To offer opportunities to develop good exercise habits, and
4. To educate employees on healthy lifestyle choices.

In the past, our DC office had a gym on the facility, and for several years we sponsored Weight Watcher programs for on-site employees. While this helped a few people lose weight and improve their personal fitness, it did not engage a large number of employees, and very few employees took advantage of the on-site fitness facility.

The HR team realized that they needed to develop a more comprehensive program that would actively engage more employees and achieve more significant results. Taking the premise that positive change cannot be achieved by imposing mandates or penalties, the Bank developed a voluntary program based on positive reinforcement and a healthy dose of friendly competition. We adopted the CALMER[2] approach from the American Institute of Preventive Medicine to develop our health and wellness program.

C—Communication
A—Assessment
L—Lifestyle Enhancement
M—Medical Self-Care
E—Education
R^2—Rewards and Reporting

With the CEO's support, we were able to earn the buy-in of senior management. Next, the HR team sought input from employees to learn the types of health-related activities and events that would interest them, to engage them personally about our initiative, and to motivate them to continue participating in the program.

The result was the voluntary Health Challenge program, launched in 2011, that included lifestyle enhancements, medical self-care, and educational programs including health-related classes and an annual health fair at the Virginia and Ohio offices, where the majority of the Bank's employees work. In the small regional offices, we reimburse up to $35 per month for gym membership for each employee who joins the Health Challenge.

Our medical self-care component teaches employees to make better healthcare decisions, to become wise healthcare consumers, and to know when to seek care. We reward employees who get an annual physical and have two dental check-ups per year. Why? Because emergency room visits, for example, greatly increase a company's medical claims expense; the American Academy of Emergency Physicians estimates the average cost of an emergency room visit is $1,349, while the average cost of a doctor's visit is $199. By regularly visiting their primary care physicians, our employees reduced their total number of emergency room visits—good news for everyone.

To add some fun—and an element of competition—the HR team built in a variety of ways to earn points and prizes. The activities for which Health Challenge participants can earn points include:

- Attending "Lunch and Learn" health classes
- Walking in groups during lunch or after work
- Complete a thirty-minute workout at a gym
- Attending Weight Watchers meetings

- Participating in events such as the Cooperative Development Race 5K or the Susan B. Komen Race for the Cure
- Playing in a baseball/softball/bowling league
- Getting a physical prior to participation in the Challenge
- Completing certain screening tests annually: OB/GYN, vision, dental, skin test, mammogram, prostate exam, colonoscopy, etc. as appropriate

Employees track their activities on a monthly basis and submit their records to HR to have their points recorded.

Each year, HR kicks off the Health Challenge at an all-staff meeting, then advertises it via e-mail and the quarterly NCB newsletter. The excitement begins with the rollout of activities and builds throughout the year as participants work to earn points.

The Health Challenge consists of three 16-week sessions. To participate in this voluntary health program, employees pay a one-time fee of $20, which helps cover the cost of the prizes that participants earn. At the end of each session, prizes are awarded to the three employees with the highest number of points for each session. All employees who participate in the Health Challenge receive a prize according to the number of points that they earned in each session. Finally, at the end of the year, prizes are awarded to those with the highest total points for all three sessions.

HR holds monthly "Lunch and Learn" sessions, where we invite outside speakers who discuss health topics such as reading labels and counting calories, diabetes prevention, cholesterol monitoring, reducing blood pressure, heart health, and meditation and mindfulness. HR also sponsors an annual all-day Health Fair, with medical screenings (cholesterol, blood pressure, body composition), free massages, and health cooking demonstrations. The Bank's health and benefits carriers are invited to participate in the Health Fair as well. These HR-sponsored events are open to all employees, but Health Challenge participants can earn points by attending them.

Participation in the Health Challenge has risen to more than half of our employees at present. This includes employees at all levels of the company, all the way from the CEO down to the mail clerks. Best of all, people have begun to invest in it; as the program has become more popular, employees have come up with new ideas for exercise classes and volunteered to lead them. One employee asked HR to buy a Step Aerobics video and now leads a class based on it. One employee is a champion runner who trains other employees to run marathons. An employee once offered "boot camp" classes with intensive cardio and strength training. Employees have also started informal lunchtime and evening walking groups. The members of these exercise groups have developed a sense of camaraderie, encouraging them to stick together and stick with the program.

The end goal of the Health Challenge program was to earn the preferred rates that insurance companies give to groups that have lower claims for health care costs. The Bank achieved this goal and succeeded in stopping what had been a steady yearly increase in health insurance premiums.

As shown in the table below, the cost of health insurance from our two providers was increasing at rates higher than 10% per year before the Health Challenge. By 2014, when the positive effects of the Health Challenge were measured by the insurance providers, NCB experienced a "negative increase" (reduction) in our NRECA medical premiums. As of the start of 2015, the reduction in NRECA premiums has persisted; NCB has earned a 0% increase on AETNA premiums as well.

Year	NRECA Medical	AETNA Medical
2015	-0.20%	0.00%
2014	-1.20%	12.00%
2013	2.47%	15.50%
2012	6.20%	10.60%
2011	15.00%	15.10%

This reduction in health insurance costs has allowed NCB to reinvest in the Health Challenge, to expand it and offer employees higher-value prizes in the Health Challenge, which has created even more excitement about the program (if they participate for two sessions, they earn prizes worth more than their buy-in). Even so, it's something the executive office is willing to do; the numbers show that the HR team has created a program that literally pays for itself.

The success of the Health Challenge program enabled NCB to meet is organizational objective: decreasing medical care costs. In addition, there has been a decrease in the number of employee sick days, further reducing our costs. Employees are more engaged because they are healthier, both physically and emotionally. Last but not least, they have an increased sense of community, camaraderie, and team spirit, in large part because of their shared participation in the Health Challenge.

Through the Health Challenge, HR succeeded in educating employees about the benefits of being proactive in their own healthcare. Employees have taken charge of matters that affect their personal health and, by extension, the health of the entire organization.

Due to the great success of the Health Challenge, NCB was recognized by the Washington Business Journal as one of the Greater Washington Area's Healthiest Employers of 2014 and 2015. That same year, NCB was recognized as one of the area's Top Employers by the Washington Post. In 2015, our Ohio office has been named one of the top employers in Ohio by the Society for Human Resources Management (SHRM) and our Virginia office was recognized again as one of the Top Employers by the Washington Post.

If you are considering establishing a wellness program in your organization, here are a few guidelines to ensure its success:

1. Establish and communicate the company's wellness philosophy, policies, and programs. Include the organization's intent, level of involvement, and rewards and incentives.
2. Diversify the components of the wellness program. Offer health assessment activities, outside activities, educational classes, individual and group programs— whatever variety you can muster. Ask for ideas.
3. Present physical and psychological health as connected issues, as different aspects of one's overall health. Aggressively address the issues that lead to absenteeism, reduced productivity, lower disease resistance, and higher accident rates.
4. Make the health program voluntary. Do not require employees to participate. Do deny coverage or limit benefits for those who do not participate. Do not take adverse employment action against employees who do not participate in the wellness program.
5. Address the needs of high- and low-risk employees in the wellness program. Include healthy risk management programs for the obese and those with high blood pressure,

disease management for those with diabetes and asthma, and catastrophic-illness management for those with cancer.

6. Engage all employees. Wellness programs that are effectively managed will not succeed without high levels of employee participation and engagement.

7. Keep it relevant. Employees prefer activities that are personalized and targeted to their specific needs and that support their work/life balance. A wellness program should speak to all interests and concerns of employees, be clearly aligned with the company's goals, and be linked to rewards that are personally meaningful to employees.

8. Stay positive. Positive approaches for improving well-being—which encourage rather than threaten and reward rather than punish—are most beneficial. When employees feel good about themselves and what they are doing, they are more likely to continue to make the right health decisions.

9. Play it safe. Organizational wellness programs should be certain they cover all bases regarding data integrity, safety, security, and regulatory compliance.

10. Make sure the program addresses all legal and compliance issues. Federal laws that apply to the design and management of wellness programs include the Americans with Disabilities Act (ADA), the Genetic Information Nondiscrimination Act (GINA), the Health Insurance Portability and Accountability Act (HIPAA), and the Patient Protection and Affordable Care Act (PPACA).

The NCB Health Challenge allowed the Bank to meet its organizational objective: decreasing health insurance costs. That success alone is cause for celebration. But the Health Challenge has given us so much more than a better bottom line: it has given all of us new senses of health, peace of mind, and community spirit.

It is easy for companies large and small to start making healthier workplaces. Begin with your employees; address their needs and learn what they want, and in improving as a result, they will in turn help the organization meet its goals. So take the Challenge for yourself!

References & Further Reading

Powell, Don R. (2014) "Twenty Characteristics of a Successful Worksite Wellness Program." American Institute for Preventive Medicine. PDF file.

Thomson Reuters. (2011) Thomson Reuters Workforce Wellness Index. Retrieved from http://healthcarescience.thomsonreuters.com/Indexes/assets/WorkforceWellnessIndex

Society for Human Resource Management. (May 2013) Designing and Managing Wellness Programs. Retrieved from http://www.shrm.org/templatestools/toolkits/pages/designingandmanagingwellnessprograms.

Michele Fantt Harris
SPHR, GPHR

Michele Fantt Harris is the Senior Vice President of Human Resources for the National Cooperative Bank in Washington, DC. A seasoned HR professional, Michele has worked in Human Resources in education, nonprofit, healthcare, and the insurance industries. Her first book, *What's Next in Human Resources* (Greyden Press, 2015) was a groundbreaking read for Human Resources professionals and entrepreneurs.

Active in many Human Resources organizations, she is a past president of the Human Resources Association of the National Capital Area and the former Black Human Resources Network. A member of the Society for Human Resource Management since 1985, she served on the Society for Human Resource Management national board from 1996 through 2001 and is a past chair of the SHRM Foundation Board of Directors.

Michele completed the Results Systems Coaching program and is an Associate Certified Coach (ACC) through the International Coach Federation and a Certified Career Management Coach (CCMC) through The Academies, Inc. A member of Delta Sigma Theta Sorority, Inc., she served on the board of the Delta Research and Educational Foundation from 2008 to 2014.

She received her Bachelor of Arts from the University of Maryland, a Master of Administrative Science from Johns Hopkins University, and her Juris Doctorate from the University Of Baltimore School of Law. A certified Senior Professional in Human Resources (SPHR) and Global Professional in Human Resources (GPHR), Michele teaches at Catholic University. Michele is a native of Baltimore, Maryland, and currently resides with her husband in the District of Columbia.

Nikki R. Jackson

Audacious HR

I love the word "audacious." It's bold. It speaks to a confidence and clarity that many of us long for in our work. It invokes a sense of courage and dogged tenacity. It's melodic. Shoot, it's just fun to say. *Audacious.*

And I adore Human Resources: the craft, the practice, the discipline. I love our roles as the keepers of human capital, the "soul" of our organizations. I love our struggle, our tension in determining to whom we are beholding, the never-ending dance to support both managers and employees, even the occasional call to "pick a side" from the internal clients with whom we work. HR will always be the human capital consciousness of any organization; sometimes we're a great example of it and sometimes, well, we suck. On our best days, your friendly neighborhood HR comrades model, espouse, produce, proclaim, celebrate and promote everything that is right about work. It's on those days that we operate with audacity.

And so, with fearless audacity, I begin my writing journey here, with each of you.

First of all, here's what largely informs my HR practice: I love work, mostly the ideals associated with work. I always have. I love watching how people work and what it does for them. I love seeing people find meaning and purpose in their work and in their workplace (two different things, but more on that later). Starting my career as a labor and employment lawyer, I learned a great deal about process and procedure and the interplay of the two; I also learned about the degradation of the two and what happens when that dynamic unravels over time at work. I've seen how work, and the places where it happens, have the ability to destroy people and sap their energy and talent—but I've also seen examples where work and the workplace affirm, validate, sustain, celebrate and nourish people. The quality of a person's work can give them life or bring them death, and it's sad that Human Resources often doesn't fully appreciate the psychology of the work dynamic in this way.

Human Resources plays a *critical* role in shaping a work environment rich with professional and personal endorsement. I understood that as a young attorney, which is why I never became an old attorney. I left the practice of labor and employment law after several years and have been in HR ever since. I've worked in public and private organizations, large and small, on the East and West Coasts, for great companies and not-so-great, for awe-inspiring bosses and hot-mess bosses entirely unburdened by tact or humility.

So, while I loved the "work" part of the traditional work environment, I infrequently loved the "environment" part. But when we discuss the ever-elusive concept of "employee engagement," as HR often does, we have to remember that both work and the work environment matter immensely. In my view, from the standpoint of both an HR practitioner and a regular employee, the traditional work environment is its own conundrum; as it is, it's fraught with cultural and behavioral norms that can make work alternately euphoric or nauseating. Either way, in order to succeed, all employees, including HR, must wrestle, at some point, with figuring out the ideal work environment.

There's often this inexplicable tension between being hired to be excellent—a change agent, an example of a new cultural norm—and actually being given the full support and latitude to operate in the fullness of your excellence. I'd say this is especially true of HR folks. This is where the traditional work environment gets to be a bit schizophrenic. Most organizations claim that people are "their most important asset," and I believe that most CEOs genuinely believe their people are their competitive anchor, but I also believe that too many CEOs continue to view the HR department as ancillary to the business. Thus, unless you want to talk payroll and benefits with them—the obvious "bottom line" stuff—there's not much to say about HR. How can this duplicitous view of HR exist alongside the belief that, in the work environment, people matter the most? It's almost as if these organizations proclaim: "Our people matter immensely, but the 'people people' among them—not so much."

My consulting practice focuses on helping HR departments do and be better. I have a fervent commitment to HR "reform"—helping to resolve that discrepancy between what HR is and what it ought to be. Sometimes though, HR can be its own worst enemy.

We may vacillate from being too people-focused—chummy, silly, or worse yet, corny and ineffective—to the other extreme, where HR teams are entirely too rule-oriented, too policy-focused, and too ready to say "no, it can't be done." We find ourselves re-covering from self-inflicted wounds—gutted, if you will, by friendly fire. "The problem with HR is that HR doesn't know it's the problem," as I was once told by an operational VP I supported. *Ouch!*

I firmly believe that our work as HR practitioners is perhaps the most critical and impact-ful role in any organization. HR is the only department, in any company, charged with building and sustaining the infrastructure that supports the company's "most valuable asset." No other department is similarly empowered or purposed. We can change con-versations, illuminate people possibilities at work, set a new course for our company's cultural ship, and reset the practice of HR—all incredibly powerful propositions. In so doing, we best position our organizations to connect with their precious people assets. We don't have to fight to be relevant—we already are. Our challenge is to stop talking about sitting at somebody's table and become potent and prolific practitioners from wherever we find ourselves sitting. We can't bemoan our CEO's belief that we are only marginally important if we fail to prove otherwise—if we lack a clear point of view on people matters and are, ourselves, profound examples of what work ought not to be. *I'm just sayin'.*

So it is HR where, for me, the transformational work begins. Our confidence, clarity, understanding of core HR practices, and ability to quickly translate our "people pain points" into actionable remedies are what matter most. We must be unequivocal about who we are to our organizations, about what we do each day that positively impacts the emotional and practical experiences of our employees. We have to be clear about why we matter so very much in reforming the way that work works, both in words and in actions. So let's stop begging for seats at others' tables and instead assure them that our work is so incredibly compelling—so game-changing and competitive-advantage-ensur-ing—that our peers, bosses, and colleagues will all clamor to sit at ours.

I first learned this lesson while working in a very public HR role. It was my first opportu-nity to lead a large team of HR professionals, more than 200 people. I was 37 years old. In December of 2007, I was appointed Personnel Cabinet Secretary for the Common-wealth of Kentucky by Governor Steven L. Beshear. Despite having been plucked from private sector obscurity, and despite the fact that I'd had no real exposure to the politics or the nuances of state government administration, I began cutting my professional teeth in public sector HR. The Governor's charge to me was to focus on the strategic transformation of HR. Prior to that point, I had spent my career dreaming about the opportunity to affect major changes in HR, to explore brand-new possibilities in work, and to cultivate an environment where all employees could do and be their best. So the Governor's direction was like music to my ears.

So for purposes of that work, and my work today, here's how I define strategic and transformation in the context of work and HR.

Strategic. What I mean by the word is simply "applying a thoughtful approach to our work with a specific end in mind." In a strategic world, HR practitioners are more than event planners, rubber stamp artists, paper processors, edict issuers, and rule owners. We are deliberate, skilled operators who understand the impact of talent management, organizational effectiveness, leadership development, and performance management, as well as how each of these concepts, if executed flawlessly, can positively impact both the employee and employer.

Transformation. This is different from "change." Change starts from what is in existence today and tweaks, modifies, or edits. Transformation, on the other hand, means bringing into existence tomorrow what does not exist today. Instead of taking matters out of the proverbial box, it assumes there is no box. Transformation in HR will challenge the way that we think about our work and the way that our customers and employees view our work. Their experiences, their expectations, and their needs must be front-of-mind for HR at all times. Being ever mindful of that basic proposition is, in and of itself, transformational.

Strategic transformation takes some time, but it need not be protracted or labored. It starts with a focus on HR's internal "brand," its readiness to adopt a posture of service (without cowering), and its ability to articulate a value statement that employees and candidates can believe in. Beyond branding, other areas to focus on would include:

- Articulating a strong but simple HR strategy statement
- Identifying and obliterating obstacles (cultural, behavioral and structural) to your transformation
- Increasing the sophistication of HR practitioners in terms of skills and content knowledge
- Instilling hope back into work and the workplace

I know firsthand that accelerated transformation in HR can be realized within the public sector because I have seen it and been a part of it on at least two occasions (after leaving Kentucky State Government, I led the HR team at a large public community college system and realized the same result). I blindly and unapologetically believe this kind of transformation is possible for both public and private entities. In my experience, even large HR systems can realize real transformation within 18-24 months; so too can your organization or most anyone focused on this work.

Take Beyoncé as an example.

It's no secret among my friends and family that I am entirely enamored with Beyoncé. To be clear, though, it's not so much her music that interests me; it's her artistry, her clarity, and her unapologetic insistence that our country's shadowy music business play on her terms. She studies how and when she is most impactful and she works her craft in incredibly progressive ways; she is an artful transformation agent. I have been drinking the Beyoncé Kool-Aid since her Destiny's Child days, all the way through her present reinvention of herself (and, in many ways, the industry) in recent years.

She released her self-titled *Beyoncé* album in December of 2013 as a complete surprise, something most artists would never do. Still, News Corp Australia network reported that Beyoncé's surprise album reached the top spot on the iTunes charts in 104 countries in its first three days; that's more than the combined opening week sales of Katy Perry's *Prism* and Lady Gaga's *Artpop*. The numbers make Beyoncé's 2013 release the fastest-selling album in iTunes history. The world's leading advertising experts say Beyoncé's album launch—with no hype or warning— was a total game changer for the marketing industry. Artists, authors, Fortune 500s, entrepreneurs, and everyone in-between is learning that social media and online marketing can only get you so far; building great relationships with your customers (or fans) is the single greatest form of marketing you can do. Beyoncé's album's release was successful "because she had a huge fan base, poured her life into her brand, and constantly displays her talent," CNBC.com reported.

For years I have been proselytizing the importance of internal department marketing— yes, even from the HR seat. Beyoncé has spent years telling her fans who she is and inviting us to share, perhaps even benefit from, her talent. HR can do the same thing. Here's how:

Clarity—Clarity begets credibility. Case in point: is there anyone who sees Beyoncé who doesn't "get" who she is, what she stands for, and how she matters to the music industry? Of course not. Similarly, within any company, the HR department, the keeper of the "people purpose," better know the same about itself. Who is the HR department to this company? What exactly does it do that makes it unique? And why does it matter so much to the organization's overall success? You must be able to articulate sound and consistent answers to these questions and assure your customers can as well. That's how you build your "fan base."

Vision—Define your department based on what it is becoming. Stop telling the world what you are and start telling them what you will be. Then, be it! The key to transformation: figure out what you want to be, tell the world you are that, then work toward actually becoming it. I have had the pleasure to serve as CHRO in three different organizations; common to each was my charge by the respective CEO to "transform HR." Critical to my work, at each place, was my insistence that HR focus inward on its own misgivings, ideology, and belief system. In each organization, HR was initially regarded, to varying degrees, as "police," "killjoys," "fun suckers," and "bureaucratic paper pushers." I would tell my team, at least 100 times a week, that "words matter." What you believe yourself to be, how you regard yourself, how you describe your work, how you invite yourself to be regarded, and how much external definition you permit will impact your success. Your organization will very much appreciate that kind of direction.

Talent—Be great at what you do and how you do it. That, my friends, is the essence of real talent. It is beyond critical, especially in a transformative movement, that you not sell a bill of goods. Now listen: I understand that, at the outset, you may not have the skills, abilities, or maybe even interest among your HR team members that you will need to really fulfill the promises of your new brand, but you must work diligently to get there. So, as a part of your internally-focused transformational efforts, you must find every appropriate opportunity for your folks to receive training—the right training. Historically, I have been a huge fan of developing homegrown HR series based on themes that undergird the principles that support your emerging brand. Those usually are unrelentingly focused on "how," not necessarily "what." While growth in your teams' technical acumen is important, meshing that skill with approachability, credibility, trust, authenticity, and a spirit of resolution, are as important. HR needs and deserves dynamic talent ambassadors.

HR Transformation is indeed an art. As you move through your transformation journey, help your team and your colleagues understand that you are in the game-changing business. You are aggressively becoming what your future requires and you are doing it from your own uniquely powerful and audacious point of view. It's more than what you know. What matters is what you can do with what you know.

Just ask Beyoncé.

Nikki Jackson

Nikki is the principal and owner of Nikki Jackson Consulting, a firm dedicated to transforming organizations one HR department at a time. She works to help accelerate the HR department's contributions, modernization, efficacy and overall restoration. Her areas of expertise are higher education and the public sector.

Previously, Nikki served as Vice Chancellor for Human Resources for Maricopa Community Colleges, the largest community college system in the country, where she oversaw all human resources functions that serve more than 10,000 employees. She led a function of more than 180 HR practitioners and is credited for the fastest transformation within the HR department at Maricopa. She modernized a 40-year old HR operation and inspired a new awakening in the HR department.

When appointed as Personnel Cabinet Secretary by Kentucky Governor Steven L. Beshear in 2007, Nikki became the youngest Cabinet Secretary and first African-American female to lead the Cabinet in Kentucky's history.

Nikki is a member of the Society of Human Resource Management, the Florida Bar-Labor and Employment Law Section, and the National Employment Law Council. She holds a Juris Doctorate degree from the University of Miami School of Law and a Bachelor of Arts degree from Hampton University.

Nikki has authored several leadership development courses and has been a featured keynote speaker, both nationally and regionally. Nikki has authored several articles on transformational HR and strategic leadership in HR and has been featured in television, radio, and print as a subject matter expert.

Nikki resides in Louisville, KY and together, she and her husband Vince have two kids, Justin and Jada.

Cheryl Jekiel

Beyond Business Partnering:
Two Factors for HR's Business Success

When considering the future of Human Resources, there are two key factors that are required for HR to do great work. The first is that the organization needs to see the HR function as a powerful component of business results, including significant impact on customer relationships. The second is that HR professionals must be able to perform well in the right areas of a business to make a noticeable difference. Yet often one or both of these factors are missing, which leads to frustration and, in some cases, failure.

Plenty of room exists to raise the standards for HR, whether in terms of their performance or the expansion and adaptation of their roles. Imagine HR rises to meet those new expectations; imagine a business climate where the most impactful department at every level of an organization is Human Resources. What would that organization's successes look like?

In short: Human Resources needs to be a critical component of not only business strategy and problem-solving, but also sustaining the culture that achieves the vision of the organization.

There is plenty of conversation about how Human Resources needs to get a "seat at the table." A great deal of the discussion around that table is missing the potential power of expertise on people that HR provides, which continually downplays the value of this field of expertise. But until HR takes their competencies and proves itself capable of producing real business results, it won't be a leader of strategy at the business table. This is why raising the expectations of HR while focusing their business acumen and skills is the formula for a HR function that makes a real difference.

Part One: Creating A New Vision for HR

Raise the Performance Bar for HR

To start, consider what is expected of the HR function. Many times, when I speak with key executives and ask them about their level of satisfaction with Human Resources in their organization, they grimace and reluctantly admit their disappointment. These leaders are waiting for stronger performance that, for reasons that elude them, seems not to be appearing in their staff.

However, moving beyond the actual HR staff (who, personally, are often near and dear to their hearts), these key executives struggle with how to make better use of the HR function. Many of them experience this dissatisfaction, but very few recognize that simply accepting or tolerating their disappointment is a big part of the problem. I'd assert that leaders' tolerance of Human Resources' failure to add substantial value is probably one of the biggest threats to its credibility.

The most common complaint from HR staff members is that they are left out of conversations, meetings, and events, leaving them strategically disadvantaged. They also complain (even if only to their friends) about feeling underestimated and underused. But when we ask the executives, "Why aren't the HR professionals included more often?" they tell us they assume HR doesn't need to be included because "nothing being discussed is directly HR-related."

This viewpoint assumes a pretty narrow range of HR-sensitive topics, as though hiring, performance management, training, and compensation were the only concerns. Making a difference to the bottom line—or enhancing the experience for your customers—requires access to a wide range of business discussions. The full capability of HR is rooted in its expertise on people: engagement, motivation, management, culture, and behaviors that achieve key performance objectives.

To give an example of this "narrow" view of HR: when a business is hiring, HR is often expected to take the "order" from the hiring manager and then fill the position according to stated specifications. As such, HR can appear clerical, mechanical even; it isn't expected to powerfully impact the organization.

So raise the standards! The service of HR needs to include commonly—not rarely—identifying business needs and detailing competencies that will create important results (sales goals, cost reduction, performance goals, whatever they may be). We need to require our HR folks to use their skills to truly impact hiring, to the point that you could trace real financial performance to the results of their actions. HR professionals can often find themselves working "down" to expectations, not up to them—a shame, as some of my best work experiences have been with leaders that demanded bigger and better results from us. It is, again, very important to set the right expectations.

Most executives that employ Human Resources don't fully understand that living down to expectations doesn't help build the confidence or experience that HR Professionals will need to contribute as fully as they can. If anything, it prevents it. Ask more of HR; in return, give them the chance to listen and to speak.

HR Professionals need to fully stand tall in their own judgment, business sense, perspective and ideas to make a critical difference.

Look for (Insist Upon) Broader Skills

Once, when I was speaking with a group of executives, they asked me: "What's the best background and training for an HR person?" The answer to this question isn't obvious, since traditional HR professionals often have backgrounds in employee relations, union relations, benefits, or compliance. Increasingly, our backgrounds are broader and include expertise in leadership, team dynamics, organizational effectiveness, and other general business acumen. Business Partner HR Professionals, in particular, are well-suited for supporting managers and teams on business goals; however, assuming that designation remains uncommon, it's beneficial to think bigger about what generalized HR expertise can bring to the table.

To start, I'd recommend that all HR staff members have some Organizational Development experience. It really engages professionals on development, performance, group effectiveness, change management, and leadership. I've spoken with many CEOs on this topic who have no good idea of what HR professionals need, in terms of background and experience, to be successful. This is an excellent starting point.

The next matter is the business acumen of the HR staff. But we're visited again by the problem of low expectations; HR professionals usually have a fairly weak business acumen relative to other departments, but then, many leaders don't expect business acumen from their HR professionals. I know many people in HR, wonderful people who are otherwise very smart, who barely know anything about the revenue base of their business, or what drives their organization's key metrics outside of HR, or even basic information about who their customers are—and they're not expected to know it. This vicious cycle, all of this information and input HR doesn't receive, limits them from realizing their full powerhouse potential within organizations. If HR's "weakness in business" is a nodded expectation, then leaders are tolerating mediocrity; for the sake of their success, they have an obligation as leaders to raise their expectations for HR and then provide them with the access and tools they need to excel at business thinking.

Part Two: HR Must Be a Business Driver

There are a number of key performance factors for creating best results. Just as someone must have a leadership vision for the work, so must the practitioner have certain tools to carry out the work well. I've found that a key element of good HR practice is setting the expectation that we will have an impact on the customers, then using a wide range of opportunities to make connections between the work we do and the real people we serve inside and outside of the organization.

From the early years of my career, in the "post-personnel" era, HR has been seen as a support function. Long ago I listened to a leading business consultant from a prestigious firm, and he said that "support functions, like HR, Finance and IT," were "dead weight" on the business— meaning that the provision of external goods and services were creating clear profit or value, while "the support functions" were simply a function of overhead.

As I listened, I made up my mind, right then and there, that my professional mission was to expand the role of HR to ensure it was adding tremendous value to business. It was obvious to me that the power of human expertise, of psychology and performance and change management, was essential to the operation of any business. HR can be a defining part of business success, and certainly far better than a drain on the business.

But how can HR drive business results? That is the question—here are some suggested starting points.

1. Amp Up HR Efforts by Touching External Customers

Amp up Human Resources by giving them the sense that they directly impact your external customers. This sometimes requires you to draw numerous connections, but to help you see the idea for yourself, the following are some ways to help make that foundation:

- As appropriate, train your entire organization about specific customer needs. If they know about customer needs, they can produce better products and services, to the point that the customer could detect when it is customized to their preferences. Whenever possible, provide examples or case studies applicable to your organization that include descriptions of those needs and other key details about the customer. Include them as part of the outcome; show them how their awareness of the customer will help them do their jobs better.
- Align your organization's employee branding with your external customer branding for a significantly stronger impact on the market.
- Get involved in projects or strategies that involve significant change. If involved in a transition, HR expertise can greatly improve business results and positively impact customers.
- Both inside and outside the company, use your knowledge of the customer (and their influence) to have your own influence on the discussion.

Once, at a session on HR thought leadership, the speaker drew "HR Strategy" and "Business Strategy" as parallel lines, to represent the way they're typically considered separate domains with separate goals. But then the speaker said, "The better way to think of HR is to remember that the line can move. It can actually push the line of the business strategy and directly drive the results." She drew the lines again, HR's a little higher; she drew them yet again, and the Business line had risen to match its growth. Ever since that day, the image of HR directly impacting the business strategy has been the prize.

2. Focus on High Priority Items

Another way to strengthen HR efforts is to look at the strategic links between (A) your daily work and (B) what needs to drive your business in the current period. Over the years, I've seen HR groups focused on what they believe are "important" HR topics—leadership training, for example. But these efforts were often disconnected from the core strategies of the business. As I spent time on the operations side of the business, the futility of this approach became clear. It's not a question of whether the programs were good or valuable; simply put, they just didn't address the greatest needs of the business directly.

Every business faces a few key challenges, and often, one will be especially large. Yet we often miss the question: what could HR really do to get past the biggest roadblocks facing the business? Applying skills and talents, understanding working motivation, and providing effective training are well within HR's domain; those abilities can support many specific strategies and will likely make a big difference by the end. This won't happen if HR expertise is not present when the most important items, or problems, are being discussed.

For example, I was once part of an organization that was struggling to make the year's financial goals. However, I knew they could very likely reach their goals if they hired a Purchasing Manager early in the year to focus on getting favorable pricing (as Purchasing had done the prior year). When I began to make this recommendation, complete with a plan, it was apparent from the looks on people's faces that they weren't used to an HR person thinking this way—in terms of results. While I could not mandate this hire on my own, I focused on gathering support for this hiring strategy, rather than simply working through the typical HR "hiring process" silently. Accordingly, more HR people need to ask themselves if their typical tasks are the best use of their time and talents.

3. Operating as a True Service Organization

A third way to improve HR is to have them approach their work as other service-based businesses do. In the last several years, a key topic in "updating" HR has been a new focus on metrics—for example, how to measure the ROI (return on investment) of training programs, or how to assess the real costs of turnover. But, again, think of HR as other service-based businesses think of themselves.

Take, for example, a hotel. When hotels take feedback from guests, they are gathering customer data on everything from check-in to cleanliness to amenities to the staff, and you can bet they track the data. But when the hotel makes changes based on the feedback, you won't hear them proclaim that "you can now check into the hotel 10% faster" or that "your room is 5% cleaner than last time." This is because the hotel is aware that, to its customers, their value is a particular kind of *experience*, which involves some attention to detail but is largely the result of attentive *service*.

Try looking at how these types of businesses use survey approaches to measure and then improve their service. Consider how some of these methods apply to HR and how this approach can be extended to all the support functions, including how they can work better together.

4. Strengthen the Teamwork of HR, Finance and IT

Building on the hotel analogy, consider how each "department" of a hotel works together to provide top-notch service. When you're in a luxury hotel, the ones known for the best service, you notice that even the maintenance staff will stop what they are doing to ensure a guest has their needs met promptly. The departments work together because they observe the principle that guests always come first and then they work as a team to uphold that principle.

When the support functions (e.g., HR, Finance, and IT) join together and ensure that their customers, the people to whom they provide service, have all of their needs met— you will see employees performing at their best and the people receiving their services rating their experience the best.

Along these lines, try using the survey practices noted above to establish coordinated "satisfaction and improvement" plans for all support function at the same time. A fully integrated approach to customer service is ultimately greater than the sum of its parts and yields the best long-term results.

5. Assess the Real Opportunity for Success

Even though there are plenty of ways to strengthen HR, it's important to make sure not to burn out by working on initiatives that aren't likely to be successful. Wishing things were true doesn't make them true. It doesn't pay to work towards success if the required elements of success are not present. And, if leadership doesn't have a vision for utilizing HR more fully, then no amount of trying can ensure HR's impact. Having witnessed many of these experiences, it's only reinforced that we'll need to become clearer about the conditions under which HR can truly deliver on its potential.

The Post-Human Resources Era

The future of HR will be driven partly by increased expectations and partly by expanding the roles HR is to play in business. In addition, HR professionals will need to develop relatively strong business and organizational development skills to be able to make a bigger impact at the table.

INCREASED EXPECTATIONS + IMPROVED PERFORMANCE = BETTER HR

To reflect these rising expectations and required performance, we'll likely have a new name for HR. Some of the newer terms, such as "Business Partnering" and "Talent Management," already reflect the outgrowth of "Human Resources" and call for something new. Someday, in the not-too-distant future, referring to "Human Resources" will be as outdated as using the term "Personnel Department." Whatever the next common term for the human aspects of a business will be, it will presume a new vision for the power of this field for empowering our professions.

Cheryl Jekiel

Currently, Cheryl M. Jekiel is the founder of the Lean Leadership Resource Center (LLRC), which sponsors a range of workshops, learning communities, publications and speaking engagements. The mission of LLRC is to promote the advancement of inspirational leadership, the implementation of Lean cultures, and the development of Human Resources Leaders.

With over 25 years of manufacturing experience, Ms. Jekiel has held Vice President of Human Resources positions for Tri-Arrows Aluminum, Inc., FONA International, Inc. and Flying Food Group, LLC. Ms. Jekiel also served for five years as Chief Operating Officer after a number of other leadership roles at a Specialty Bakery in the Chicagoland area. Ms. Jekiel has developed an expertise in Lean manufacturing with a particular focus on Lean cultures. Ms. Jekiel has made countless significant improvements in reducing operating costs and leveraging a Lean culture to obtain new business. Ms. Jekiel brings a tremendous passion for continuous improvement in her commitment to building Lean HR as a recognized field of work, and to that end is the author of *Lean Human Resources: Redesigning HR Processes for a Culture of Continuous Improvement.*

Maurie McGarvey

The HR Coach:
Leading Others by Leading Yourself

Many people believe an organization's culture is the key to its success, and typically the most-desired culture is one in which employees are truly engaged. Would you agree? Might you also agree that leadership sets the example for employee engagement? After all, as the leader goes, so go the others.

"Engagement" is one of today's biggest buzzwords in business, and there's a lot of noise surrounding the topic. Google search results are endless and varied; thousands of "experts" real and self-proclaimed are writing about it and making money consulting on it. But we can't make engagement happen from the outside in; it cannot be forced or required, but instead has to be invited. This is the key premise that HR leaders, coaches, and other "people people" forget.

When we are tasked with improving workplace factors as deeply personal as engagement, we are required to dignify what makes each person's experience different. Each of us brings our perceptions, beliefs, and life stories into the workplace every single day. Our level of engagement is determined by these unique experiences, yet HR and others have often wrongly assumed that everyone demonstrates engagement in the same way.

As HR coaches, we simply guide others on a path of continuous improvement and growth, creating an environment for people to remain engaged and self-aware as we go. But can we lead others effectively without first committing to lead ourselves along this path?

I. Self-Leadership

The key to effectively coaching and leading others is to first effectively coach and lead ourselves. Simply stated, self-leadership is the ability to motivate yourself. It sounds easy, and as we'll discuss shortly, it can be. But first, we have to understand that the key to successful self-leadership is conscious choice.

Conscious choice provides an awareness of why you think the way you do and awareness of who you truly are (as opposed to who you've been told you are). Consider the idea that we are always leading, whether we are consciously choosing to or not. If we are not choosing how we lead—if we are "leading by default"—we are allowing our past experiences and judgments to set the tone and expectations for employees. If we are choosing how we lead, we are intentionally guiding ourselves in a specific new direction.

Intention is the energy behind the messages we tell ourselves. These messages pre-cipitate our actions and determine how often, and how well, we "show up" in our lives. When you are leading yourself from a mindset of awareness, you engage others differently than when you're on autopilot, not leading yourself. As you learn to choose your responses to the world consciously, you create the way you lead . . . and you start to create the world in which you want to live.

The key to self-awareness is recognizing what you can control and what you can't. Re-member that, at every moment and with every experience, we can consciously choose our responses; that is something we control almost completely. When we are leading ourselves consciously and effectively, we understand this; then, we are able to lead others toward the empowerment and engagement that stems from their re-discovery of this principle. Then, as a result, employees will be in the best position to put their personal resources to use and start kindling their own leadership potential.

II. Recognizing Who You Are Being

We've all heard the phrase, "If we want different results, we need to DO things differ-ently." What if I told you that, if you want different results, getting them has far less to do with what you do differently, and everything to do with how you think? If we want a different experience, we need to think differently. We must choose our level of awareness of our thoughts and feelings, which drive how we act. Because of our strong cultural focus on measuring results in all aspects of our lives, we have developed the habit of "doing" rather than of "being." We more typically find meaning in tangible things, which are fully present and easier to judge.

Who you are being is an ongoing conditioning process, and it is occurring at all times. Becoming conscious of this conditioning and recognizing how you are changing over time, and how that compares with how you want to lead, will give you the rare insight to know where you need to go next.

We view the world through filters: our experiences, our assumptions, our interpretations, and our values. We also experience the world in multiple dimensions: physical, emotional, mental, spiritual, and so forth. Our experiences ultimately lead us to develop our own version of reality. No one else has lived your life; no one sees the world quite the same way you do; no one knows what you know, sees what you see, or thinks what you think. Be quick to identify and check your perceptions and assumptions. How "true" are they really, and how are they affecting your achievement of your goals? What if you made a different assumption—how would that impact your results? Take time to notice how your thoughts create the feelings or emotions that then drive your actions. Our degree of awareness creates the world we experience, moment by moment. By shifting our interpretations, our assumptions, and our perceptions, we create a more engaged life for ourselves and set a more engaged leadership example for others.

The ways in which we currently lead originate in life experience, from what we already know. Reflect on who you are currently being, or how you are currently "showing up." What beliefs and opinions have brought you to this place? How have those beliefs and opinions affected your life? We are typically disengaged when we are preoccupied by the past or distracted by the future; we miss the opportunity to "show up" in the moment.

To focus on the moment, practice "detached involvement" in which you are both a participant and an observer of your life. While observing, you regard *all* experiences as important for your growth and development, and you place no judgment on them as being good or bad. You are in control of how you respond to them. In this state, you can choose not to take anything personally, to avoid making assumptions, and to let go of the need to be right—among other ways of leading ourselves to the best outcomes.

So now, with a clearer picture of self-awareness, ask yourself: when you reflect on how you spend your energy, how much of it is focused on trying to do things differently to achieve a different result?

III. Being Your Mission

We often segment our lives into the roles we play or the titles we assign ourselves: employee, spouse, parent, friend. We attempt to build walls around our personal lives and our professional lives, creating an expectation that one shouldn't affect the other. This is simply an unrealistic expectation. We are whole beings, not just separate roles bound together, and it's very easy to confuse our roles with our mission. Think of it this way: if you no longer had your job title, who would you be? Would your team still follow where you lead them?

It's essential to understand your personal mission; it's important to your role as an HR leader and professional. It makes a significant difference in the workplace and makes you more effective as an HR coach. Again, as whole beings, when our values are not being served in one aspect of our lives, other parts of our lives will be impacted, as will the people around us.

To be your mission, you first have to be perfectly clear about what is truly important to you. When you think about what you value most, reflect on how those values are being served in your life. Remember that values are also products of our experiences; values drive us, but sometimes they reflect what we were taught to want more than they reflect what we actually want.

For example, you may place the highest value on creativity, or service to others, or integrity. You may value adventure, or privacy, or spending time in nature. No matter what carries the most meaning for you, you will find yourself more engaged when that value is being fulfilled. When you are feeling as though your values are not being honored, it's important to assess why that is. Are you ever in situations that run contrary to your values? Do you surround yourself with people who reinforce your values or people who oppose them? How does being an HR leader feed your mission? How are your values being honored as an HR leader? An awareness of why you feel blocked from your values leads to a sense of empowerment over removing the blocks.

How do you remember what your mission is? Examine what motivates you and gives you a sense of purpose. Here is one approach which may help.

1. First, list three things you want most out of life.
2. Next, list three things you want to experience.
3. Then, list three things which make you unique.
4. Finally, identify three things you can do to positively move forward.

You can then combine your lists into a statement like this . . . "I can _4_ using my _3_ to experience _2_ and also achieve _1_." Try it and see if it helps to provide focus for you. The clarity may help you identify what you want to change in order to feel more aligned with your mission.

When you are clear about your mission, how can you then connect with it? First, be keenly aware of your strengths and talents. Know what motivates you; notice when you feel invigorated. Honor your hopes, dreams, and desires. Assess what your unique experiences have prepared you for and what they have taught you. Finally, envision what your ideal life would look like.

Think on what feels right in your life. What is working? What is possible? What opportunities lie within perceived setbacks?

IV. Moving Forward

You are, at this moment, the culmination of your unique life experiences. Yet you have the opportunity to change your thoughts in this moment so you may begin to lead yourself on a more authentic, more engaged path. And if you are completely unique, then it stands to reason that every other individual is as well, wouldn't you agree? If we consider that every person we meet is also a unique blend of whatever formed them in life, then we can begin to remove judgments in how we experience others. We can recognize that we each form our own version of what is "true" for us, even if it doesn't align perfectly to the absolute Truth. When we understand the difference, we are able to motivate others simply by our presence, in having power without forcing. Power is inspiring others from within themselves; power is in being rather than in doing. The ripple effect will impact your organization in meaningful ways you may not anticipate.

In essence, leadership of others is creating influence in others, whether we can observe that influence or not. So every interaction we have with others presents an opportunity to lead. Think about your personal definition of leadership: when was a time you embodied that definition? What strengths did you draw on to make it happen? What made others follow you?

Showing up as your most authentic self draws others to you. There is nothing you need to do to force that. When you are consciously choosing how to be, you will naturally lead others toward meeting their own full potential. HR coaches recognize that creating an organizational culture of engagement begins with our personal engagement in the lives we are creating for ourselves.

Maurie McGarvey
SPHR, SHRM-SCP

Maurie McGarvey is the Senior Vice President, Human Resources Director for the Paducah Bank & Trust Company in Paducah, Kentucky, and is celebrating her 20th year as a Human Resources professional, most recently adding corporate and executive coaching to her areas of expertise.

Maurie is a certified Senior Professional in Human Resources through the Human Resources Certification Institute and a Senior Certified Professional through the Society for Human Resource Management. She is a past and upcoming member of the Kentucky Society for Human Resource Management State Council as well as a past president of the Four Rivers SHRM chapter in Paducah, Kentucky.

Maurie is a Certified Professional Coach and an Energy Leadership Index Master Practitioner through The Institute for Professional Excellence in Coaching, which is accredited by the International Coach Federation and the Human Resources Certification Institute.

Maurie graduated from Western Kentucky University with a degree in Paralegal Studies. She also graduated from the Kentucky Schools of Banking Bank Management School and the Graduate Schools of Banking Human Resources Management School.

Maurie is active in the business and arts and culture communities in Paducah, provides Human Resources and coaching expertise to the various non-profit agencies on whose Boards of Directors she serves, and has been recognized on a local and state level for her leadership and volunteerism.

To contact Maurie, find her on LinkedIn, email her at maurie@paducahbank.com, or call her at 270.575.6623.

Jeff Nally

Rally the Courage to Coach:
Rethinking HR's Strategic Role

I love teaching people how to have coaching conversations. It's rewarding to see others generate new thinking when they respond to powerful coaching questions. But, as an experienced Human Resources professional, it's most rewarding to me when I can teach these skills to HR colleagues so that they can lead with greater influence and impact. In the pursuit of that reward, there have been a couple of shocking surprises.

I was recently honored to teach 100 Human Resources professionals, my colleagues in a Fortune 100 company, how to have coaching conversations with leaders in their businesses. I explained the brain-based approach to coaching, taught coaching conversation skills to them in small groups, and helped them practice their new skills. At the end of the training, I asked the participants two simple questions:

1. Are you confident that you can use the coaching skills you learned?
2. Do you have the courage to lead coaching conversations with business leaders?

To the first question, almost 100% of the workshop participants said "yes." They had confidence in the use of their newfound coaching skills. Obviously, I was pleased with this result. It aligned with what I'd seen in them during their instruction and group coaching sessions.

But to the second question, only 50% of the participants said "yes." Meaning that half of them admitted that they lacked the courage to lead coaching conversations with business leaders—does this surprise you? As a coach and company colleague, I was shocked! Really, *only half* could muster the courage to have a coaching conversation?

At first, I didn't believe the feedback. Was it really possible that these professionals, my HR colleagues and friends, just didn't have the will to ask coaching questions? This confused me; I'd seen them making strong cases with business leaders, standing up for HR processes, and calling for real changes in their organizations. I spoke with people individually and gathered feedback in small groups—but my questioning only confirmed the results. After that, I could only wonder: why did they lack the courage to coach?

Let's reimagine HR's strategic role as "courageous coach."

The Many Hats of HR Professionals

Human Resources professionals wear many hats. This is to say that we play many different roles to meet the needs of employees, leaders, and the organizations we serve.

We wear the "consultant hat" to diagnose problems, determine root causes, and point leaders towards solutions. This is an important hat to wear, as the organization depends on HR to be the content expert in all matters related to people practices.

We wear the "manager hat" when we lead people or build their skills to accomplish things on their own. For example, HR trains managers and employees on the company's performance review process and enables them to lead the process on their own. This is an important hat to wear so that we help make everyone as capable as they can be.

We wear the "mentor hat" when we use our position, experience, and depth of knowledge to help others. For example, we may mentor new managers or anyone who is new to Human Resources as a field. We guide people with less experience and foster growth in future leaders with this part of our work.

While all of these "hats" are important, there's one hat that can transform HR's impact and influence more than all others—and that's the "Coaching Hat."

When to Wear the Coaching Hat

When HR wears the Coaching Hat, we take on a role that is different from all the others. We lead a meaningful conversation by asking coaching questions. Coaching conversations are most useful when the leader doesn't have a clear answer or has underwhelming solutions for the problem she is facing.

For example: a leader needs a new customer relationship management (CRM) system, but there's no budget available, and the IT review team put the request on low priority due to other demands. The leader doesn't know what to do next. This is a prime opportunity for HR to lead a coaching conversation to help the leader think through possibilities.

Coaching conversations are also useful when the stakes are high and there is risk involved making a decision. Coaching conversations help the other person consider several options and make an informed choice before moving forward.

Another example: a leader decides to update job descriptions to meet the changing demands of the business. There are several implications for training and developing the current workforce, and there are challenges recruiting new hires that meet the updated qualifications. HR can wear the Coaching Hat to help the leader examine her thinking and her approach—before then putting on the "consultant hat" to help her implement the new job requirements.

Coaching Conversations, Not Coaching Engagements

Coaching conversations are moments when asking questions can be more strategic and impactful than lecturing, consulting, or mentoring. Coaching conversations last a few minutes, not hours. Coaching conversations are not the same as a coaching engagement that can last several months, follows a process of self- awareness and goal-setting, and is led by a qualified, certified coach.

Coaching conversations include brain-based coaching questions and some of the competencies that certified coaches use. HR professionals can help leaders generate their own insights, ideas, and approaches to challenges in the workplace, and whenever it is needed. Remember that, in Human Resources, you coach for the needs of the moment, not the needs of a lifetime.

Asking Coaching Questions

The key difference between wearing the Coaching Hat and wearing other hats is inquiry: asking questions that spark the other person's thinking. These questions often focus on the leader's goal or ultimate outcome, whether or not the leader knows how she'll get there.

The key to coaching conversations is to keep questions focused on the goal or desired outcome, not the current problem. When we focus on the problem, the emotional center of our brain goes negative, defensive, and inhibits new thinking. When a leader experiences a problem, coach the leader through the following:

Seeing the Goal Realized—Goal questions may include asking the leader:

- What does the end result look like to you?
- What does success look like to you when this is resolved?
- Describe what's happening or what exists when you achieve the outcome you want.

Answering these questions creates neural maps in the brain, connecting neurons with the images and descriptions of success. Leaders need strong neural maps to stay focused on the goal, especially when challenges arise.

Reflection and Self-Awareness—After the goal is clear to the leader, coaching conversations should continue with questions that prompt self-reflection and self-awareness. The leader should next focus on what she really wants, rather than think about the problem.

When the leader reflects on her thinking instead of the problem, the emotional center of her brain shifts to neutral or slightly positive emotions. She focuses her attention on current and future states of achieving the goal that's important to her. All of this allows the part of her brain that generates new ideas—the prefrontal cortex—to be ready for an insight or new moment of clarity that can resolve her problem.

Here are some examples of questions that invite self-awareness and reflection:

- Describe your current thinking. Is it foggy or clear?
- What makes it feel foggy or clear for you?
- How do you think about this goal, relative to the way you usually think about them?
- What are possible first steps that get you closer to your goal?
- Picture this goal fully achieved and realized, then look back to today. What's the next step that got you closer to realizing this goal?"

These are thinking questions, not problem-solving questions. The result is insight—that "aha" feeling, new ideas, and clearer options for moving forward.

Momentum to Take Action—Now that the leader has some new ideas, the coaching conversation capitalizes on that momentum to move forward. Her brain is ready to consider options, make a decision, and formulate next steps towards realizing the goal. She is more likely to act on her intentions because now she is generating her own new thinking.

Some questions to capitalize on this moment, create momentum, and build confidence:

- Which option for moving forward are you ready to pursue?
- What are the steps you know you'll need to take to move forward?
- Who is involved in those next steps? Who can help you?
- What resources will you need going forward? Do you have easy access to those resources? If not, what needs to exist so you can access those resources?
- When do these next steps need to begin? When do they need to be completed?

HR professionals can have confidence leading these conversations because they are based on neuroscience, on proven coaching competencies, and in an easy-to-replicate process. It's why almost 100% of my HR colleagues said they had confidence in their new coaching conversation skills. It's not voodoo; it's built on proven science. It can be learned. But the problem, as we've seen, is not lack of knowledge; it's lack of courage.

Rally the Courage

Human Resources professionals can have the skill, yet still lack the courage to lead coaching conversations. I learned that some HR professionals didn't have the courage because the people they support don't expect the HR partner to ask questions. To the contrary, they expect HR to give answers all the time.

HR can rally courage by setting some expectations with the leader she supports. When mentioning the "different hats" that HR wears, go ahead and tell leaders that you're adding one more hat to the mix. Set the expectation that HR should lead a coaching conversation when there is a problem, when no clear answer is available, or when the stakes are high.

When it should happen, ask permission to lead the coaching conversation so leaders and employees aren't surprised or confused when HR takes a few moments to ask thinking questions instead of consulting or mentoring. Rally courage by setting expectations and letting people see you wear the Coaching Hat.

Another way to rally courage is to experience a moment of success when the leader has a new idea or insight as you coach her. If you have ever been around someone who has an "aha" moment, you remember how her face lit up. After that, she will lean further into the conversation and be more ready to take decisive action.

The more you see this change in the people you coach, the more you become an "insight junkie" and start looking for chances to lead these conversations and help others break through to new ideas and solutions. The pleasure centers of your brain light up as you experience the positive impact you have with others.

Advancing the HR Profession and Your HR Career

People in your organization will begin to notice that they're solving tough problems because of your help. You are the one who put on the Coaching Hat and were willing to invest a few moments to ask some questions that helped leaders to solve their most troubling problems.

You will be respected and sought-after to help the organization think through difficult situations, yet you don't have to be an expert on each problem. You can set aside the fear that you don't have all the answers—in a coaching conversation, you're not supposed to have the answers, only good coaching questions.

Human Resources has come a long way over the years. We stepped out of the comfort zone of "functional" HR and started seeing our potential to engage employees and create wonderful places to work. We mustered the courage to play different roles to fulfill our commitment to serve employees and the employer. But these evolutions took time to understand and acts of courage to validate, and now we are at another turning point in our profession when, to play the role of the coach, we have to remember to be brave.

Let's eliminate any of my shock and surprise in the future—fifty percent of HR professionals shouldn't lack the courage to ask coaching questions with business leaders. You can help leaders think differently so they can move the organization forward; you just have to be willing to start the conversation. So rally your courage to coach—then, when you're the most insightful new person at their table, you'll be realizing the new dream of what the Human Resources profession can be.

Jeff Nally
SPHR, SHRM-SCP, PCC, RPCC

Jeff Nally creates expert neuroscience applications for leaders, HR professionals and executive coaches. He is a speaker, executive coach, author, and leader developer who crafts brain-based solutions to improve leaders, teams and organizations. Jeff is the president of Nally Group Inc., a practice that brings results with the brain in mind to leaders and organizations.

Jeff has 23 years of professional experience in Human Resources, executive coaching, and leadership development in corporate and not-for-profit organizations. He is a certified Senior Professional in Human Resources (SPHR) from the Human Resources Certification Institute and a Senior Certified Professional from the Society for Human Resource Management (SHRM-SCP). He is a past chair of the Kentucky SHRM State Council and a past president of Louisville SHRM. He is the inaugural recipient of the Lyle Hanna Volunteer Spirit Award for his volunteer efforts to advance the HR profession.

Jeff is also a Professional Certified Coach (PCC) through the International Coach Federation, a Results Professional Certified Coach (RPCC) through Results Coaching Systems, and a certified StrengthsFinder Performance Coach through The Gallup Organization.

Finally, Jeff is a nationally-recognized speaker who applies neuroscience and coaching to help people solve business problems. He is a frequent speaker at business, coaching, and Human Resources conferences across the US.

Jeff holds a Bachelor of Arts in Psychology from Georgetown College in Georgetown, Kentucky, and a Masters in Business Administration from Georgia State University in Atlanta.

Contact Jeff at Jeff@NallyGroup.com, 502.810.4116, or at www.NallyGroup.com.

Dave Phillips

Start at the Front Door

Earlier this year, when Cathy first invited me to contribute to this anthology, I was preparing for a long-overdue vacation with two of my sons. This vacation was meant to be a time of contemplation for me; I had been considering retiring from my current career for almost a year, but now I would have time to weigh my options.

As that vacation approached, our HR team was working to convert our job application process from hand-written to 100% electronic. Applicants would be able to submit the paperwork online. After that, we only had to provide the system with the right criteria and it would do the rest—the applicants would be analyzed and weighted, the interviews scheduled, and the best candidates highlighted. As someone who started an HR career in the late nineties, before the Web and personal devices were so ubiquitous, this process amazed me. It also caused me to look back on my careers and to reflect upon what I'd learned through all that time.

I've always been a "lucky" person, but luck definitely runs both ways. One of the bad turns, or so I thought, came when I received a draft notice from the U.S. military—the final draft of the Vietnam War, no less, and I received it only a few days before the birth of my first child. I was a "hell no, I won't go!" anti-war type, so I decided not to report for my induction physical. A visit from local law enforcement helped me to revise that decision quickly; presented with the grim alternative, I became a member of the United States Army through the Kentucky National Guard. (Ironically, my initial distaste for the Armed Forces didn't passto my sons; Jeremy retired from the Army after 20 years of decorated service and Zachary is currently in his 10th year of commitment.)

On Valentine's Day of 1973, I reported to the reception center at Fort Knox, Kentucky. I left behind my young wife and newborn son. Reluctant, but resigned to my fate, I decided to try and make the most of the opportunities there. Fortunately, the Army had just introduced their new training program—six weeks of Basic Combat Training and six weeks of Advanced Individual Training—which was better-suited to make civilians battle-ready and competent as team members. My Drill Sergeant gave me my first leadership role: platoon guide for my unit of 32 men. The responsibilities were modest—maintaining headcount, assigning small tasks, and reporting information to my superiors—but it was the first real leadership role I'd had since finishing high school.

I learned early that "leadership" was not as much about "standing at the front" as it was about listening to others, dignifying their concerns, and giving them sound advice based on whatever knowledge and experience I had. However minor the difference seems, I was a 20-year-old among kids who were 17 and 18; I was a voracious reader; I was married and a father; I'd had a little more "life experience" than most of them. They listened to me. If I was a good leader, it was because they respected me, not because I tried to stand taller. I eventually gathered that this willingness to serve others was a God-given trait that, if developed, provides its own satisfaction to the person serving. I found it in the military, and I knew I wanted to continue cultivating it when I returned to civilian life.

When I returned home, I resumed where I had left off, in masonry and construction with my two brothers and my father. We worked hard and the profits were good for most of the year—but the seasonal nature of the work was taxing, and working as a self-employed contractor without medical benefits was especially troubling after the birth of my daughter, Stephanie. Especially given the depleted housing market of that time, I was worried that I wouldn't be able to provide my family with what they needed.

So I reached out to an uncle, an HR manager at a local company. While he couldn't hire me because of company policy, he was able to refer me to a peer at another company. I took the resulting entry-level job at York International in their HVAC assembly plant. What a change—a paycheck every week, medical benefits, a company-sponsored retirement program, and 600 co-workers from all around the area. It was a dream come true! They even paid overtime, something I hadn't been able to expect while self-employed—and it was encouraging to see that, in this place, all I had to do was give an earnest effort in my work. My energy came naturally.

My first Team Leader was an older gentleman who took an interest in my enthusiasm. He was the first to encourage me to bid into other departments and learn all I could. He told me he believed I could be a great manager someday as long as I didn't forget one basic tenet: that I should listen to the people that support me and recognize them at every opportunity.

I took his advice. I moved to other areas of the plant. I learned process flow, developed good relationships all over, and eventually applied for a management opening in my department. I lost out to one of my peers, who had a few years' more experience—which was discouraging, until the following Monday when I was notified that my peer had second thoughts and turned down the position. It was mine if I wanted it! I happily took it—but I knew that I would have to prove that the decision to promote me was the right one.

I did what I had learned to do: I focused on the people. I learned what they liked and didn't like, how they spent their time and energy away from work, what made them different as people. I managed their work and tasks, as was my job, but I also took the time to speak with them every day. In so doing, I was always able to praise what they'd done well and critique what they hadn't. We had friendly competitions between shifts. As all of this was happening, we were breaking production records every month, and the pride that people took in their work was only getting higher. They were able to work as a team and accomplish big goals together, even if they accomplished them in small ways: "shooting" screws, wiring units, labeling the products. They identified themselves as a Team and took pride in it, and it made our work better.

But one night in 1991, after the close of the late shift, I had to help the Shift Manager hang a sign over the gates of the facility announcing its closure. It was over—just like that. Hundred of people were suddenly out of work because of the business decision to relocate the manufacturing to other facilities. The employees of our plant would be considered for re-employment only if they were willing to move hundreds of miles to one of the other plants. This news was devastating to us, but it was out of our control.

I weighed my options. I interviewed at other facilities in Oklahoma, Ohio, and Houston, Texas, which is where I wound up moving to serve as a production line manager. My wife and two-year-old son, Jacob Ross, would join me there by the end of the year.

This was a new chapter with a new challenge. For the first time, I had to learn how to manage a multicultural workforce, and in a new facility no less. In addition to my daily responsibilities, I was included in the development of the new employee handbook (which is where I developed my first real interest in Human Resources). We were in start-up mode: 12 hours a day, 7 days a week.

Once again, I was tested to use what I'd learned. I made friends across that cultural divide; I learned more about the Hispanic community and their families and their work habits. The same principles I'd applied before were now being tested across a cultural boundary—and they worked the same as before. Just by showing that I care about more than the job, I was able to make the job better (and made some good friends besides). Now, too, I was able to make a bigger difference with what I knew—my leaders truly listened to my ideas, and what I knew about our multicultural workers affected both the content and phrasing of the materials in our company policies and handbook. I saw again that, while these relationships take time to develop, they have hundred-fold returns with the loyalty, engagement, and winning attitude that they engender—and the results can be permanent if leadership understands that.

That chapter, too, came to a sudden end when I was diagnosed with Systemic Lupus. During treatment, I was chemically depressed and thus, totally disabled. Given the probability that I would not return to work in the near future, we decided to move back to Kentucky to be closer to our families.

Treatment didn't produce many positive results. My medications (and their dosages) were being changed constantly. I was gaining weight due to non-activity and the side effects of my prescribed medication. I was at the bottom of the barrel—and with a return to my faith, I realized that the only way to look was Up, and I laid my condition at the foot of the cross. I went cold turkey on my medications against my doctor's advice, but I'd decided to take my chances with God. I'm not a fanatic, but I'm a believer—and I've had no major setbacks in the twenty years since.

With my health and energy on the rise, I sought full-time employment again. I received an offer from a local plastics manufacturer and met with the HR Manager, who asked if I could start immediately. I said yes, but added that my daughter's wedding was the coming Saturday and that I would need the afternoon free to attend it. The HR Manager told me that was "unacceptable" and that I would be required to work if I wanted the job—so I walked away. My own shock and anger aside, I couldn't work for a company that wouldn't show such considerations for their employees. If nothing else, the occasion had been a sharp reminder of my basic principles and why they make a difference, so I took my insights elsewhere. (Coincidentally, that plastics manufacturer closed its doors less than a year later.)

I wound up taking a salaried position with the Plant Manager at Hudson Foods, a new poultry processing plant, in June of 1996. Once again, I had to become familiar with the process, which in many ways was the reverse of the assembly plants I'd seen before (at Hudson we took units apart and created pieces, whereas in manufacturing you take pieces and put them together to create units).

Over the next two years, I was promoted through two levels of management. All throughout, I did the same basic things I'd done everywhere before. I communicated thoroughly and honestly with people, I answered questions, I praised earnest effort, I held people accountable in caring ways. I knew the people who worked with me. In small ways, they were able to see that I really cared, both as a person and as a member of their team. The song remains the same.

In 1998, Tyson Foods acquired Hudson Foods. During the first year of transition, I applied for the Plant Human Resources Manager position. I knew that my skills would be a major benefit in that role, and my urge to get into a Human Resources role was hungry, almost obsessive. Less than a year later, I was promoted to Complex Human Resources Manager.

The first task assigned to my team was to become active in the communities around us. A third-party poll organized by community leaders showed that we had a 21% acceptance rating in the neighboring area. We took the principles out into the public. We began meeting with community groups, getting involved in community projects, giving attention to community concerns, and donating to local civic and charitable organizations. A follow-up poll two years later conducted by the same community officials showed that we'd earned an acceptance rating of over 80%, a massive improvement.

All we did was listen to the people we serve and respond to them. We started to dignify people's problems. We took the time to educate the ignorant, to communicate openly and clearly, and to show up, to be seen and recognized.

In the last five years especially, our nation has become a potpourri of culture. In the little town of Robards, Kentucky, at the Tyson Foods Complex which has over 1450 employees, minorities comprise nearly 45% of the workforce, and today's workers come from more than 40 different countries and speak more than 20 languages. Communication barriers are always present, and there are promising developments towards addressing those problems (another topic for another anthology), but the first priority of a leader is to know how to listen to their people, through any interferences.

As HR professionals, we have a responsibility to all levels of the companies we work for. But too many times, we see an emphasis on coaching our managers—which, while important, shouldn't overshadow the needs of the many workers below them. We can't ignore 96% of the workforce—the portion actually providing the efforts and creating the products—while we focus all of our attentions on the 4% that manage the different levels of the business.

If you want to make a difference, Human Resources professionals, live your own people principles every day. Be there when they get to work. Talk and listen to the people you work with, every day. Tell them when you appreciate their efforts. Visit them at their workstations and in the break rooms; find ways to make yourself available and get managers to do the same. Find out what makes each person happy. Lastly, remember to spend time acknowledging what people do right, just as you spend time addressing what people do wrong.

And when it comes to communication barriers, remember one thing: no matter where you come from, no matter what language you speak, everyone understands a smile.

When it comes to serving people, start at the front door. Don't be afraid to walk up and extend your hand.

Dave Phillips

Dave worked in the family construction business prior to spending over 17 years with York International as a Product Line Manager in Madisonville, Kentucky and Houston, Texas. He recently retired from Tyson Foods, Inc. after over 19 years where he served as the Complex Human Resource Manager of the Kentucky Complex for the last 16 years.

Dave also served in the Kentucky Army National Guard for over 14 years. He received his certification as a Professional in Human Resources (PHR) in 1993 and served on the Executive Board of the Owensboro Society for Human Resources Professionals for seven years, holding the offices of Vice-President, President and Past-President. Dave has been a member of the KYSHRM State Council for ten years and is currently serving an extended term as the Western District Director.

His community involvement has been decorated with over 15 years of serving the communities in the tri-state area, being appointed to seats on various Chambers of Commerce and other non-profit organizations. His interest in working with people from various cultures around the world has motivated him to continue to work as an advocate for refugees adapting to the culture changes they face in America.

Labor relations is another field that Dave has a passion for and will be available for consulting services in October 2015. He can be reached at wdavephil@gmail.com or via LinkedIn.

Laura Hlavacek Rabideau

HR in the Mirror:
Reflecting Upon Implicit Bias from the Inside Out

Michelle looks at me from across my desk, tearful eyes revealing her hurt and anger. Working to keep my face straight, I wrestle with my own confusion, not sure what to think about her accusations, much less how to make matters right. How did we get to this place? I know I don't understand all she is telling me, all she is feeling, and that bothers me. How am I supposed to help her navigate a difficult situation when I'm not sure I can even understand her perspective? What am I missing here?

Michelle has come to see me a number of times over the past few months. She is a young African-American woman and a consultant, and she's been struggling with her manager, a white man in his mid-fifties. And, at this moment in my career, I'm her HR generalist, a 30-something white woman, busy untangling what seems like a series of miscommunications.

Michelle told me about a client meeting when her manager relegated her to taking notes. Michelle, offended, felt he only asked her because she is the sole black woman on the team. I listened, but I thought that this couldn't be the reason. Her manager was a good guy, I knew, a sought-after team leader. Regardless, their relationship was on the skids, so I sought him out to get his side. He was offended by her reaction and explained to defend himself: "She is the junior member of the team. When I was the junior member of the team, I took notes too. It has nothing to do with her race or gender." This explanation made sense and seemed reasonable to me. Then I decided it must be a simple miscommunication, easily remedied.

I share this conclusion with Michelle, certain that this will get them back on track. But then I see Michelle deflate and begin to sense her growing frustration and hurt. "Laura, I'm telling you. It is based on race. I know it. I feel it. You wouldn't understand." Frustrated myself, I realize I am missing something. There is something here I've failed to see, failed to understand. Worse yet, I've failed to help because of it.

We—HR folks—joke about how our jobs would be easier if we didn't have to deal with people. But at the same time, I've always felt we secretly love the complexity and the messiness of working with human beings, especially when we feel like we are helping, when we're making a difference despite the messiness and complication. At that moment, though, I didn't feel like I was helping Michelle at all. So what was I missing?

Perhaps this situation feels familiar to you—or in general, the sense that there's something about another person that you can't grasp. This is largely a function of *implicit bias*, or our tendency to subconsciously act on our assumptions about people different from ourselves. I didn't realize at the time that this was a factor at all, but now it's clear to me that its impacts are pervasive and its potential effects profound for organizations.

Implicit biases shape our view of the world and influence how we engage with others in all areas of our lives, including as HR professionals. This, it turns out, is what I was missing in my interaction with Michelle. Until I could learn to reflect upon my perspective and see around corners in new ways, I was always going to miss something in conversations like the one with Michelle—and I'd therefore be missing something in the effort to build a diverse and truly inclusive work environment.

I've been driven by a passion for this profession. I love the challenge of helping people bring their whole self to work; I love coaching managers to become inspiring leaders; I love learning the business intimately so we can get the right people focused on the right things. Especially recently, we HR professionals have worked hard to build our business acumen, develop deep technical expertise, and become trusted advisors. We have earned a seat at the table. We have arrived, and I couldn't be more thrilled about that. But we have a responsibility as Human Resources, and that responsibility is to leverage our access and influence to reshape the culture of inclusivity for the organizations we serve. To do this effectively, we must first understand the real impact of implicit bias and how it impedes our best work as inclusive organizations.

To start simple, we can define bias as "a preference for one thing over another." The tricky part isn't when we are talking about a preference, say, for Mint Chocolate Chip ice cream over Rocky Road, or a preference for Jimmy Fallon versus Jimmy Kimmel. The tricky part is when bias refers to an unfair preference or prejudice.

Perhaps the word "bias" makes you feel uncomfortable in this context—"implicit" does make it all the more painful to consider. "Implicit," after all, means that we have feelings and attitudes beneath our awareness that aren't always identified through self-reflection. Implicit bias helps explain how we process the mountains of data our brains process each day, as well as why we notice certain things and miss others. In large part, that's all dependent upon what our subconscious notices, and partly also, this is an inherent property of the way we're wired. Bias, a preference for one thing over another, provides the foundation for our beliefs about the world and drives our decision-making. It is necessary for our survival, since it helps us to quickly assess threat or opportunity, to distinguish friend from potential foe.

What if we acknowledge that it exists and has persistent effects? What if we could shine a light on our implicit bias and consider how it impacts us as HR professionals? If there were a way for us to become aware of these unconscious preferences, we could short-circuit the effect that our implicit bias has on our thinking and decisions. This is not an easy task simply because everyone has their own lens on the world, their own implicit biases to sort through. However, as we begin to explore the influence of implicit bias upon our work in HR, there are a few key characteristics of implicit bias that you should keep in mind (source is the Kirwan Institute for the Study of Race and Ethnicity):

- Implicit biases are pervasive. Everyone possesses them, even people with avowed commitments to impartiality such as judges.
- Implicit and explicit biases are related but distinct mental constructs. They are not mutually exclusive and may even reinforce each other.
- The implicit associations we hold do not necessarily align with our declared beliefs or even reflect stances we would explicitly endorse.
- We generally tend to hold implicit biases that favor our own ingroup, though research has shown that we can still hold implicit biases against our ingroup.
- Implicit biases are malleable. Our brains are incredibly complex, and the implicit associations that we have formed can be gradually unlearned through a variety of debiasing techniques.

Are you wondering if you have any implicit bias? You do. (So do I. We all do.) Over 20 years of data from the Implicit Association Test (IAT) confirms that implicit bias is just part of being human. Researchers at Harvard, the University of Virginia, and the University of Washington launched the IAT, which measures the attitudes and beliefs people may not be willing or able to self-report, by testing the strength of associations between concepts such as young or old, gay or straight, black or white, with evaluations or stereotypes.

For example, my test results show that I associate men with better math skills than women. I would tell you, and sincerely insist, that I believe men and women are equally capable at math. Yet somehow, beneath my awareness and ability to control, I have a bias that men are better at math. Given my IAT results, I am uncomfortably confronted by the fact that I might, without being consciously aware of it, show preference or bias to male candidates for Finance jobs, for example. As an HR professional dedicated to creating a diverse and inclusive—and fair—work environment, I have an obligation to try and overcome thought patterns like these.

Still not certain? Don't take my word for it. Harvard's Project Implicit provides multiple versions of the IAT online and it has been taken by millions of people. Put down the book and take the test yourself at:

https://implicit.harvard.edu/implicit/takeatest.html

How'd you do? Remember, the good news is that implicit bias is malleable—we can take action to diminish its impact.

Reflect and Explore

The first step is introspection. Reflect on your feelings about inequity and how to align your conscious, explicit values with your implicit attitudes. Ask yourself some hard questions about what influences your decisions about people; try to notice patterns. Are there similarities in people you hire or select? Who do you automatically seek out for key assignments or projects? Be suspicious of your automatic responses, but remember that they tell you something and that you have the ability to change or modify them. Armed with this insight, seek experiences that can shift or reverse the patterns of experience in new directions. Conscious and deliberate effort is required to see a different perspective.

Shortly after my interaction with Michelle and her manager, I had a series of opportunities to put myself in the unfamiliar territory of being the only person "like me" in a room. On one occasion, I attended a conference focused on LGBT issues in the workplace; people spoke candidly about the stress of deciding whether to talk about a same-sex partner when a straight colleague asks them "did you have a good weekend?" As it turns out, I'd be one of those people who would cause this discomfort, even if unintentionally. *Ouch.* That is never my aim; that's not who I am; I'm an ally! But again, I had to wonder: could my own implicit bias factor into the image I project to others?

When branching out to get involved in employee resource or affinity groups, I sometimes found myself the only white member, feeling out of place where I was and, at times, feeling unwelcome. Were people really looking at me and wondering why I was there? Why did the woman explaining the focus of her successful African-American market research firm comment to me that "we don't shop the way you do"? Do I shop the wrong way? However she intended it, I knew then how even a small comment can make someone feel excluded from the group.

I eventually realized: if it feels this uncomfortable to be the only person like myself in the room for just a couple hours, what must it feel like to come to work and be that lone example every day? I kept asking myself what I was missing or not seeing, but having that insight helped me to see and appreciate multiple perspectives, as I hadn't been able to before. By having experiences outside of my in-group, I started developing some cultural competency, a more global mindset, and the ability to better put myself in someone else's shoes.

For yourself, seek out information that opposes the implicit preference you would like to change. Interact with people who provide experience that counters that preference. Remain alert to the implicit preference and recognize that it may intrude into your judgments and actions. However small, do things consciously to compensate for known implicit preferences. And when going out into the world, know that when you look least like others around you and are at your least comfortable, you are likely learning and growing the most.

The bigger question now must be: how do we, as strategic HR advisors, illuminate implicit bias embedded within the practices across our organization?

Ask Questions

We bring this new perspective and awareness of implicit bias to our role as HR professionals. We can ask questions that shift perspective.

When I was head of HR for a law firm, a senior partner came to me for advice on selecting an associate for a three-week, out-of-town trial. Courtroom experience is a potential game-changer for a young attorney. The male partner shared his thinking and said, "Kate would be terrific. She's ready and really knows the case. But she has little kids at home. I want to be sensitive to that. I'm going to ask Tom to handle it."

I replied with one simple question: "Why don't you ask Kate first?" Kate wanted the opportunity, she was ready (as he knew), and she had childcare and family support in place. (Ironically, Tom was the early morning caretaker for his young children while his wife completed her medical residency.) To be fair, the partner who posed the question to me had good intentions and thought he was doing the right thing—but simply being in the room and posing a simple question in return made all the difference.

Take Action

Here is where all the ground we have taken as HR strategic advisors comes into play. We leverage our relationships, knowledge, political savvy, and social capital to reshape HR systems, policies, and processes to ensure they are fair and inclusive. We lead our organizations to take definitive steps to root out implicit bias from our management of human capital.

Run the numbers. Look at participation across demographics in mentoring programs, promotion rates, turnover trends, performance ratings, and engagement scores. If we find differences across different groups, we should ask ourselves why those differences exist and make needed changes.

Develop programs to support diverse talent through hiring and training. We are in a unique position to partner with leaders to ensure that all types of talent receive skill-enhancing work. Identify, support, and collaborate with other programs and organizations to increase diversity in the pipeline. For example: establish clear, objective interview criteria to combat the feedback that a candidate "just isn't the right fit."

Demonstrate inclusive behaviors and encourage open discussion with colleagues and leaders about differences. A reverse-mentoring program creates opportunities for leaders to engage in dialogue with someone who sees the world through a different lens, history, and set of experiences and can help to shift their implicit biases. Recognize the impact of informal social networks and take the lead in finding opportunities to champion individuals of different backgrounds. Increasingly, organizations are investing in implicit bias workshops and training as effective ways to shift behaviors.

The impact of implicit bias on individuals and organizations is deep and complex. There are a multitude of resources and research available through organizations such as SHRM, Diversity Best Practices, Project Implicit, and consulting groups specializing in this issue. If we expect our leaders and organizations to deliver on our promise of an inclusive work environment, we need to first confront our own personal hidden bias which excludes others beneath our knowing.

"You must truly understand what makes you do things or feel things. Until you have been able to face the truth about yourself, you cannot really be sympathetic or understanding in regard to what happens to other people."
—Eleanor Roosevelt—

Before I considered the impact of implicit bias on my work in HR, I was missing a critical piece of the puzzle. I saw employees who felt devalued, discouraged, excluded. Yet I couldn't see why. From my perspective, it all seemed fair. We had policies. We had programs. The playing field was level—wasn't it? When I began to develop my own awareness, I was changed. There was something there I hadn't seen before. Changing my mindset was the first step towards expanding my ability to create a more inclusive environment within the organizations I help to lead.

I will never fully know what it is like to be the only person like me in the room every day of my life, beyond my experience as a woman in corporate America. But as a Human Resources professional—and as a human being—I deeply believe that we thrive when we have a truly welcoming workforce, and for that I will continue to work, both in the open and upon myself.

Laura Hlavacek Rabideau

Driven by the belief that successful companies are filled with successful people, Laura Hlavacek Rabideau prizes the Human Resources profession as one defined by helping people thrive.

Spanning her career as Human Capital Leader for a Fortune 100 healthcare company, Director of Human Resources and Diversity at an AMLAW 200 law firm, Chair of a national professional association's Committee on Diversity and Inclusion, and Board Member for arts and educational not-for-profit organizations, Laura embraces the challenge of creating spaces where all voices are heard and all talents valued.

Laura fostered her creativity and insight amidst obtaining a double degree in music and psychology during her undergraduate years at Northwestern University and her business acumen while earning her MBA at the Kellogg Graduate School of Management. A Chicago native, Laura has traded in the bustle of the Loop to rescue her wonderful husband in keeping up with three fantastic teenagers in Louisville, Kentucky.

Bob Smith

Earning Our Slice:
HR, Operations, and Corporate Culture

Like many of us, my first job in high school was at a local fast food chain in my hometown. Even though it was my first job, I decided then that I would make a career for myself in restaurant management. I didn't really have the means or support to attend college, but I knew the money could be good in this business—and I understood that, with time and determination, I could advance my career. I entered a management training program making $273 a week, got married, and started a family. I moved quickly through the company since I treated it like a career and not just a job, and since I'd taken to heart what I'd learned from my mentors as I matured in the restaurant business.

As long as I'm thinking back on that time and what I learned from those wonderful people, I may as well stop and give them credit for making me a better professional today. Gail Wise taught me the importance of believing in yourself. Mike Beckmann showed me the importance of looking at Human Resources differently and acting differently within the field. Special honors go to the late Pete Sechak, my longtime Area Manager and friend, who taught me the importance of managing others well, helped me understand passionate leadership, and lived his principle of treating others the way you would want to be treated.

Eventually, I was promoted to the position of Multi-Unit Operator. What that means, in the context of the restaurant industry, is that your hours are long and your work is hard—but what most people don't see is that your pay and rewards can be excellent. Despite the difficulty, I enjoyed the work—and I believe restaurant management is still a great career choice for someone who demonstrates great leadership and motivation to manage others, by the way.

I have owed many thanks to my wife Barbara and three sons, Derek, Brandon, and Connor, for their understanding and patience. There were times when I missed birthdays and holidays because, in the restaurant industry, it is very typical for managers to work nights and weekends to fill gaps and do whatever has to be done. So there were some costs to my job—and as much as I enjoyed my work, I knew something was missing. I wanted more. I wanted to have a bigger impact on people.

I made the decision to leave the company where I'd worked for over 20 years and accepted an offer to be a Field Human Resources Director for Papa John's. Fortunately, it turned out to be the best career move I could have made for my family and myself. Frankly, not many restaurant companies would have taken a chance hiring a restaurant operator to work in Human Resources, but Papa John's understood what the advantages of that experience were. To this day, I will still staff (or recommend staffing) a Field Human Resources position with someone who has an Operations background. As a professional who crossed over, I can tell you why, and maybe then we'll be Rethinking Human Resources.

What we do in Human Resources at Papa John's may differ from your usual Human Resources department at companies of a similar size. We're an incredibly lean staff, for one difference, and for another, we've reached far outside of our HR comfort zone to form relationships across every department in our company.

Taking me as an example for our HR staff: my background allows me to understand the operations side of our business and how it relates to Human Resources. The necessary skills of leadership, communication, passion, decision-making, and driving for results are all very transferrable from one to the other. But I've found that one big difference between Operations and HR is that operators are very direct—no sugarcoating. Some people find an operator's forwardness refreshing while others can be taken aback; I make it work, mostly by trying to understand my audience. By knowing what we have in common and how we differ, we can always communicate on level terms across departments.

When I was promoted in 2012 to lead the Human Resources department, our Founder, Chairman, and CEO, John Schnatter, told me that as Papa John's had grown over the years, Human Resources had been a "pebble in his shoe." He described to me a period early in the company's growth when the Human Resources department was always the first group to say "no" to new ideas, to say that we couldn't do it "that way," to say that we shouldn't reward team members at the level they were being rewarded. John knew what he wanted and how to get there: by rewarding our restaurant general managers and celebrating their successes. That was his goal for the company's culture, and it wasn't being fully realized. He then told me that he was confident that, after all these years, he had found the person that could take our culture to the next level, a restaurant operator like myself who believes that operations team members are critical to the business' success.

No pressure, right?

At that moment, I began developing a long-range plan for how our HR department could support restaurant operations in the way our senior leaders needed. I had three main goals:

- Create efficiency by removing inefficiency,
- Build trust between Operations and Human Resources, and
- Build on our corporate culture to create the best place to work in Kentucky.

Before I discuss how I have worked to make those happen, let me give you some context, both with my path through Papa John's and with the work that was already underway there. In 2007, I was promoted to the Senior Director of Field Human Resources to lead that team out of our corporate headquarters in Louisville, Kentucky. It was the second-biggest decision of my career, this time because I was moving my family away from our hometown to Louisville.

Efficiency was one of our first priorities five years before I would even lead the department. Today, we have an HR staff of 30 for a total of approximately 20,000 corporate team members. That's about one HR staff member for every 700 employees, and for most companies our size that's very lean. If we were going to be successful, the first thing we had to rethink was HR efficiency.

We needed to become an operationally focused department, but what exactly does that mean? First, we needed to update the systems and processes that supported the field operations teams. As an example, Papa John's already had an electronic hiring process—

we implemented it in late 2007—but what about the 100,000 paper applications our restaurants still collected annually? Many of the restaurant managers had difficulties and questions through the transition to a fully electronic system. How do you review applications and schedule interviews in the system? What do you do with their identification, and do they still need to photocopy it? The concerns went on and on, and as time passed I realized that this process felt like removing the training wheels for the first time—or perhaps flying a plane for the first time. To be fair, these can all be frightening transitions, but they're necessary.

Meanwhile, we were making other changes that, again, added complexity. In 2008, we implemented an electronic applicant tracking system with the onset of becoming an affirmative action employer by opening a company-owned-and-operated restaurant on Fort Bragg Military Base in North Carolina; as a government contractor, we were then required to comply with Executive Order 11246. These decisions, while challenging for our restaurant teams at the time, were focused on getting HR to understand and address the needs of operations and to make things easier in the long run. It was all about removing obstacles, removing the pebble in the company's shoe—not about what we wanted as a Human Resources department.

But what's so different about Human Resources at Papa John's? It returns to the goal of efficiency; with so few resources available, we needed to conduct business more efficiently and work only on those projects that truly impacted restaurant operations and supported the vision of our Founder and Executive Leadership Team. In order for my group to be successful, we needed to become trusted *partners* in the business. We needed to earn respect; before we said "no," we needed to be proactive about solutions that could work for everyone; we needed to truly collaborate, to attend other department meetings and represent our internal customers; we needed to support the business' growth through succession and career planning all the way down to the manager level. In other words, we had to become the culture champions across the company and work on aligning the company's goals from top to bottom.

There are so many Human Resource professionals that claim we "need" a seat at the table. It's time to move beyond that. We need to *earn* that seat. I wanted my team to truly become business partners with our executive team. Coming from restaurant operations, it was easy for me to become part of the conversations, but not so much for my team, so

I had to teach them the importance of understanding our business model. That is what gains you credibility at the table.

Thus, my second goal was to get my team involved. I asked that they attend weekly department meetings held by other groups so that they could better understand what their internal clients in other departments need. I even went as far as asking them to work a shift in one of our local corporate stores so they could better understand the business at the ground level. As some of you know, there is no better way to understand the struggles of a restaurant manager than to stand in their shoes.

By understanding our internal customers and their needs, I believed we could better support our culture. I've mentioned we operate with a lean staff. That is the case in several other departments also, mostly because we can manage it well. We have the ability to make decisions quickly, especially given that our Executive Leadership Team only consists of ten people (including John Schnatter). It is not unusual for someone to have an idea, run it by a few key people, then present it to our team and have a decision made quickly. This part of our company culture is important because it is how we operate on a regular basis, but it can be difficult for those who prefer to move more slowly or need lots of information to make decisions. Also, the manner in which we expect our team members to be accountable and the ways we interact with our vendors can be a bit different from most companies our size. So we needed a way to educate our team members about the Papa John's way.

Several years ago, John Schnatter wanted to create a leadership development program based on his experiences in the business over the last 30 years. It was our job, over the course of a year, to put his thoughts into practice by creating a leadership development program we now call "Go Left."

The title for the program came from a decision Schnatter made on the day of his father's funeral. He came back to Mick's Lounge and stood in the doorway; should he go right and sit at the bar and have a beer, or should he go left and finish building the dining room that would become Papa John's? You can guess what happened. For me, this program was the real beginning of building trust and becoming true partners in the business, my second long range goal for HR. This wouldn't have been possible five years before; it took time, patience, and persistence to build that level of trust.

It was important to me that my team be included in meetings, projects, and planning. Sometimes, we found out by accident about a project moving forward, for example, or we heard about a planning meeting in which we hadn't been included. This wasn't an intentional exclusion of HR; there had simply never been a practice of including HR in these cross-functional meetings or projects.

Once we'd broken through to them, however, there was no turning back. Teams wanted to involve us because we had so much to offer. Given the nature of our HR role—and our appearances seemingly everywhere around the company—we knew more about other departments than anyone else. Now we had immediate credibility, and it enabled us to move forward with other measures that were important for the efficiency of other departments. Today, it is not uncommon to hear someone at Papa John's say, "Let's get Human Resources involved. They can help us get that done." I am very proud of my team for breaking down those old barriers within the company.

With two of my long-range goals on the right path, it was time for us to address our company culture. We had a good culture generally, but it was inconsistent across our subsidiaries and internal departments. As a company, we hadn't publicly told our story, aside from the bit about John's Camaro and his first restaurant.

Our first step was to expand our main recognition program, which at the time was called "Slice of Appreciation." We met as a team to think about pulling all of our recognition programs under one name to help shape our company culture. Shortly after, John came to see us one day, very excited about a person he had met at another company's annual operations meeting. She worked for an internationally renowned recognition and awards company and was there because she'd helped brand that company's recognition programs. I guess it was fate that we were meeting with her.

Over the next 18 months, a cross-functional team led by Human Resources created a new recognition program called "Ingredient You." The team, with the help of a new vendor, created an online recognition platform that is used across all our company groups, and it is specifically designed for ease of use all the way down to our hourly restaurant team members. We were also able to create a program called "The Founder's Club," which encompassed not just restaurant operations, but our campus team members and PJ Food Service as well. At the end of each year, we recognize the top nominated team members with a trip outside the U.S., including the opportunity to be the overall Founder's Club Award winner for Papa John's.

What I am most proud of, when it comes to "Ingredient You," is that it was once again a cross-functional partnership born from a single idea. We heard and discussed the idea together, and then we came together to accomplish it. We were efficient in our work, but more important, we were connected together in it, everyone from HR to Operations to the Executive Team.

This is a key distinction of how we do business at Papa John's. It's also how, over the last four years, the Human Resources department has gone from being a "pebble in the shoe" to a trusted business advisor to our CEO and Executive Leadership Team. John Schnatter often says that "we're not just in the pizza business, we're in the people business," and whether those people are Papa John's customers or Papa John's team members, we believe in it. While our HR model may not work for everyone, it has enabled us to focus on what truly is most important to our success: our people.

Bob Smith

Bob Smith was named Senior Vice President, Global Human Resources for Papa John's in May 2014. Bob is responsible for directing all facets of the Human Resources department both domestically and internationally for Papa John's including Compensation, Benefits, Organizational Development, Talent Acquisition, Employee Relations, and HR Information Systems. This position plays a critical role in driving the company's culture, as well as formulating and aligning key HR initiatives in support of business growth and strategy, to position the organization as an Employer of Choice. Bob recognizes that quality, at every level, is embedded in the culture of Papa John's and fundamental to its success.

Prior to joining Papa John's in 2003, Bob spent more than 20 years in restaurant operations with KFC in the Northeast Region. He holds a Bachelor of Science degree in Business Management, specializing in Human Resources from the University of Baltimore and a Professional in Human Resources Certification from the Society of Human Resources Management.

Bob was awarded an Evanta 2014 Top 10 Breakaway Leader Award for senior HR executives, has been featured in Profile Magazine, and was a member of Consero's 2014 Chief HR Officer Forum. Bob and his family reside in Louisville, Kentucky where he serves as a Board Member for the Salvation Army, St John's Center for Homeless Men, the Louisville Zoo Foundation Board, and the Louisville Youth Training Center. Whether he is training for a marathon or volunteering his time, Bob knows that preparation and accountability are essential to his personal success.

Libraries@Trocaire

CPSIA information can be obtained
at www.ICGtesting.com
Printed in the USA
FFHW02n1259060818
47677061-51296FF